Listening Mat

Practice Tests for the London
AS and A2 Music Listening Papers
based on *The Essential Hyperion* 2

David Bowman
and
Paul Terry

SCHOTT

Mainz · London · Madrid · New York · Paris · Tokyo · Toronto

ED 12730
ISBN 1-902455-08-8

Acknowledgements

The authors and publisher would like to thank Hyperion Records Ltd for
kindly granting permission for this book to be based on their anthology
of recorded highlights, *The Essential Hyperion 2* (HYP20).

Each of the tests in this book is based on these two compact discs which
together provide more than two and a half hours of music.

The complete works from which the extracts are taken are available from Hyperion Records Ltd.
Titles, catalogue numbers and other details of these are given in the CD insert booklet.

We would also like to thank Dr Hugh Benham, Chief Examiner in Music to London Qualifications (Edexcel),
for his generous advice during the preparation of this book, and to Wendy Lampa of Schott & Co. Ltd. for
her enthusiastic support for the project. Thanks also to William Dore, for transcribing Marini's *Sonata a quattro
tromboni*, to Pat Dye of the British Library Lending Division for her help in locating a number of rare scores,
and to William Lloyd of BBC Radio 3.

CD track timings

Timings printed in this book indicate the elapsed time from the start of the relevant track, as shown on the visual display
of most compact-disc players. For example, 1'07" means one minute and seven seconds from the beginning of the track.
If you listen to the recordings on a computer-based sound system you may notice small discrepancies in these timings, as
some replay software will include inter-track silences as part of the overall track length.

Also available

Aural Matters, A Student's Guide to Aural Perception at Advanced Level by David Bowman and Paul Terry (Schott & Co. Ltd, 1993),
with accompanying anthology of 154 extracts of recorded music: ED 12430 Book with two compact discs.

Aural Matters in Practice, Advanced tests in Aural Perception based on The Essential Hyperion by David Bowman and Paul Terry
(Schott & Co. Ltd, 1994): ED 12441 Book with compact disc.

Readers are also referred to *Sound Matters* by David Bowman and Bruce Cole (Schott & Co. Ltd, 1989), an
anthology of 72 extracts of printed and recorded music, available with teacher's manual and pupils' questions:
ED 12351 Score, ED 12352 Teacher's manual (with pupils' questions), ED 12353 Two compact discs.

British Library Cataloguing-in-Publication Data.
A catalogue record for this book is available from the British Library.

ISBN 1-902455-08-8

ED 12730

Typeset by Musonix Typesetting
Cover design by Geoffrey Wadsley
Printed in Germany S&Co.7553

Contents

Introduction

IMPORTANT: details about the London music specification in this book are believed to be correct at the time of going to press, but the current requirements for the examination should always be checked with London Qualifications (formerly Edexcel) as these may change.

AS Music

The Listening Paper for AS Music is a 45-minute test that you will sit in May/June of your AS exam year. It consists of the four questions described in chapters 1–4 of this book. The music for each question is recorded on compact disc and will be played to you a fixed number of times, as described in those chapters. This Listening Paper accounts for 15% of your total mark for AS Music.

A2 Music

The Listening Paper for A2 Music is taken in May/June of your A2 exam year. It, too, is presented on compact disc and it consists of the three questions described in chapters 4–7 of this book. Unlike the AS test, you will be given your own copy of the CD which you are allowed to play over headphones as many times as you wish in the time allowed for the paper (which is 60 minutes from 2004 onwards). Each extract is recorded only once, so you will need to be familiar with the controls of your CD player in order to locate and repeat individual tracks. This Listening Paper accounts for 15% of your total mark for A2 Music. You will need to pace yourself carefully in order to have time to do justice to all three questions in the paper. Note that the final question is worth more than half the marks for the entire test – so make sure that you don't linger on the first two questions. In fact, it may be wise to tackle question 3 first.

Practising for the Exam

Each chapter in this book deals with a separate exam question. This layout will help you study for the tests during your course, but in the weeks before the exam you will need to practise working complete papers. Your teacher will have some examples to use, but you can also practise complete papers from this book by selecting one example of each question from the relevant chapters. For AS, play each track the specified number of times, leaving one-minute gaps after questions one and two and two-minute gaps after questions three and four. For A2, pace yourself carefully, using our recommended timings.

The Extracts

In the exam the extracts will come from pieces that you are unlikely to have studied, although the features of the music should be familiar from your study for the tests. The recorded examples on the accompanying CDs encompass a broad range of music. The selection is not comprehensive and other styles could be used in examinations – although most questions are likely to be similar to the ones given here. Examples of other styles of music, along with many exercises to help you improve your skills in melodic and rhythmic dictation, and in the recognition of keys, chords and cadences, are included in our earlier publication, *Aural Matters*. A few of our illustrations are taken from the CDs that accompany that book and the CD that accompanies its companion, *Aural Matters in Practice*.

1. Timbre and Texture

This is the first question on the AS Listening Paper. You will hear two unrelated passages of music, for which no notation will be provided. Each will be heard **twice**, with 30-second silences between playings. You will be asked to identify various features of the timbre and texture of each extract.

Timbre

Timbre is a French word, pronounced *tam-brr*. It means the tone colour of a musical sound. For instance, a flute and a trumpet playing the same pitch can be told apart because each has a different timbre.

You may have to identify standard orchestral instruments from the woodwind, brass, percussion and string families. If you need to brush-up your knowledge in this area, see if your school, college or local library has some recorded compilations of instrumental sounds to use for practice – Benjamin Britten's famous 'Young Person's Guide to the Orchestra' is particularly useful as it also includes instruments in various combinations and a number of special instrumental effects.

You may also have to recognize instruments such as the recorder, saxophone, harp, acoustic guitar, electric guitar, bass guitar, drum kit, electronic keyboard, piano, harpsichord and organ. You could also be asked to identify some of the more common instruments (such as sitar) and instrumental combinations (such as gamelan) heard in non-western music. In this last category, the recordings of numbers 58–63 in London's *New Anthology of Music* (*NAM*) will provide a useful guide.

Much of this will be familiar from your work in GCSE and before, but check that you do not have any gaps in your knowledge. For instance, can you distinguish the dry, wooden sound of the xylophone from the bright, tinkling timbre of the glockenspiel's metal bars? Can you tell the difference between the sound of a saxophone and a high bassoon? If you hear the sound of plucked strings, can you decide whether it is a guitar, harp, harpsichord or a group of violinists plucking instead of bowing?

Most instruments can produce a variety of timbres. For example, listen to track 20 of the second CD that accompanies this book and compare the bright tone of the clarinet's high notes at the start of the extract with the rich, oily sound of its low-register notes, which can be heard at 1'25" on the same track.

Instrumental effects and techniques

Pizzicato is an instruction to pluck the strings. Listen to bars 32–48 of *NAM 3* (starting on page 44), where violins and cellos are played *pizzicato* at the same time as violas are played with the bow (*arco*).

Double stopping refers to playing two notes at the same time on a string instrument, as in bars 217–229 of the solo violin part in *NAM 1* (page 19) and in bars 72–95 of the solo viola melody in *NAM 3* (pages 48–53). Chords of three notes ('triple stopping') and four notes ('quadruple stopping') are also possible.

Col legno ('with the wood') is an instruction to tap the strings with the wooden side of the bow. All of the strings play *col legno* at the start of *Mars*, from Holst's *The Planets* (most music departments will have a recording of this famous piece).

Harmonics are produced by touching a string very lightly so that when it is bowed or plucked a high, pure sound is produced. You can hear violin harmonics at the end of the percussion variation in 'The Young Person's Guide to the Orchestra', accompanying the final notes of the xylophone. (*Col legno* strings accompany the castanets solo in this same variation.) Harmonics can be played on the harp (see bars 167–189 of *NAM 3*, starting on page 61) and on the guitar, where they produce a gentle, bell-like timbre.

Tremolo. One type of *tremolo* is produced by fast up and down bow movements on a string instrument. This causes rapid repetitions of a single pitch, creating the rustling sound that can be heard in bars 11–19 of *NAM 5* (pages 88–90). Another type of *tremolo* is produced by quickly alternating two different pitches (rather like a trill, although the two notes are often not adjacent). This type of *tremolo* can be heard in bars 94–99 of *NAM 5* (on pages 114–116 of the New Anthology) and can also be produced on woodwind instruments (e.g. the clarinets in bar 95).

Vibrato refers to the small, rapid undulations in pitch used by string and wind players (and singers) to warm their tone – listen to the violin solo on *CD1 track 8* of the CDs that accompany this book. Note that some musicians prefer to use little or no vibrato when performing early music, as in the violin solo on *CD2 track 2* of the accompanying CDs. Examples of vibrato on the trumpet and clarinet can be heard in the recording of *NAM 48* (which starts on page 461 of the New Anthology).

Mutes can be used to change the timbre of string and brass instruments. For instance, compare the sound of a muted solo viola in the last seven bars of *NAM 3* (page 65) with its unmuted sound in the rest of the movement. Listen also to the body of muted (and later tremolo) strings in the first 30 bars of *NAM 5* (which starts on page 86 of the New Anthology). Strings tend to sound duller (and quieter) muted, whereas a brass mute tends to make the sound thinner. Several different muted brass timbres can be heard in bars 7–19 of *NAM 43* (page 375) and in the recording of *NAM 49* (page 465).

Glissando refers to sliding between notes – a technique that can be used on many instruments, including the trombone (*NAM 7*, bar 2 on page 154) and the harp (*NAM 47*, bar 79 on page 456).

Flutter-tonguing involves rolling the letter R while blowing a wind instrument – there is an example in the flute, oboe and trumpet parts at bar 105 in *NAM 43* (page 385).

Finger-picking is a term commonly used to mean plucking strings individually on instruments such as the guitar, rather than strumming the fingers across a group of strings. So, for example, the guitar players use finger-picking at the start of *NAM 56* (page 501).

20th-century composers devised many other, sometimes extreme, ways to modify timbre. For instance, *NAM 10* (page 166–170) requires the strings of a piano to be modified ('muted') in different ways by placing various rubber and metal objects between them to change their timbre. *NAM 11* (pages 171–175) requires the human voice to be used in a number of experimental and extreme ways. Treatments of this sort are often referred to by the 'umbrella' expressions of 'extended instrumental techniques' and 'extended vocal techniques'.

Singers and vocal techniques

You should be prepared to identify the following vocal ranges: soprano, contralto, tenor, baritone and bass. The distinction between the last two can sometimes be unclear. However, the lowest part of *NAM 32* (pages 344–346) is obviously written for basses (it descends to E below the bass stave and never rises as high as middle C). In contrast, the singer on *CD2 track 21* of the CDs that accompany this book is clearly a baritone – the vocal part ranges from E♭ above middle C downwards for an octave, so the singer's lowest note is almost an octave higher than the lowest bass notes of *NAM 32*.

A useful word for describing the average range of a part, especially a vocal part, is **tessitura**. The vocal part in *NAM 38* is written for a tenor voice, but it uses a very low *tessitura* throughout all of page 361.

You will need to be able to differentiate the timbre of a treble (a boy's voice) from that of a soprano (a female voice) even though both have much the same range. Compare the trebles who sing the top part in *NAM 32* (page 344) with the sopranos who sing the top vocal part in *NAM 28* (page 288).

You may also need to differentiate between two other voices with similar ranges – the female contralto (as heard in the second movement of *NAM 28*, page 296) and the male counter-tenor (as heard in *NAM 33*, page 347). The counter-tenor voice (also known as the male alto) is produced by an adult male singer using the vocal technique known as **falsetto**.

We have already mentioned that vibrato is an important technique for singers. Can you hear how it is used in the song on *CD1 track 21* of the CDs that accompany this book? Listen especially to the longer notes at the ends of each phrase. Here are some other techniques that you may encounter in vocal music:

A **syllabic** setting of a text is one in which every note (or virtually every note) is sung to a separate syllable, as in the opening of *NAM 26* (page 266). The opposite of a syllabic setting is –

A **melismatic** setting, in which a group of notes is sung to a single syllable, as at the end of *NAM 26* where there is a melisma in each of the three inner parts at the top of page 269.

Parlando means to sing in a style that resembles speaking – listen to *track 17* of *Aural Matters in Practice*, especially the sections that are reported speech, such as lines 3–4 and 7–8 of verse three. **Recitative** is a type of vocal music that is often sung in a *parlando* style – listen to the first 25 seconds of *CD1 track 4* of the accompanying *Hyperion* CDs, in which two sopranos 'converse' in recitative.

Sprechgesang means 'speech-song' – half spoken and half sung – as in *NAM 40* (page 364).

Vocalising means singing to vowel sounds rather than to words, as in the first three bars of *NAM 47* (page 440). Closely related to this is the jazz-singing technique called 'scat' (singing to nonsense syllables) which you can hear in bars 31–42 of *NAM 48* (pages 462–463).

Musical ensembles

You may also be asked to identify standard combinations of instruments or voices, such as:
- symphony orchestra (e.g. *NAM 43*) and the usually much smaller chamber orchestra (e.g. *NAM 2*),
- brass band – an ensemble that consists of a wide range of brass instruments, usually with percussion,
- military band (or wind band) – an ensemble of woodwind, brass and percussion,
- jazz band – both the traditional jazz band (e.g. *NAM 48*) and the larger big band (e.g. *NAM 49*),
- rock band (see *NAM 53–57*),
- world music ensembles (see *NAM 58–63*) such as gamelan,
- ensembles that use 'original' (i.e. period or authentic) instruments, such as the consort of viols heard in the recording of *NAM 13* or the group of early instruments heard in *NAM 27*. Such performances can often be recognised from a combination of factors such as strings playing without vibrato, crisp articulation in fast movements and the presence of instruments such as the harpsichord and lute.

Chamber music ensembles that you may encounter in the Listening Paper could include the:
- duet (e.g. two melody instruments, or one melody instrument plus piano),
- string trio (e.g. violin, viola and cello) and piano trio (violin, piano and cello),
- string quartet (two violins, viola and cello),
- string quintet (two violins, two violas and cello or occasionally two violins, viola and two cellos),
- piano quintet (piano and string quartet),
- clarinet quintet (clarinet and string quartet),
- wind quintet (usually flute, oboe, clarinet, bassoon and horn).

In most baroque music there is a *basso continuo* – a part from which available bass instruments (such as cello, double bass and/or bassoon) would play, and which would also be used as the basis for improvised harmonies by players of chordal instruments such as the harpsichord, organ and/or lute: see *NAM 36*. Also in baroque music you may come across the trio sonata – a work written on three staves (hence 'trio') for two melody instruments and *basso continuo*. Four performers are generally needed for a trio sonata since two instruments (one bass and one chordal) perform from the continuo part, as in *NAM 15*.

Vocal ensembles include choirs of mixed voices (sopranos, altos, tenors and basses), traditional cathedral choirs consisting of boys and men (trebles, counter-tenors, tenors and basses), groups of female voices (sopranos and altos), male-voice choirs (tenors and basses), backing vocals (as in *NAM 53*) and groups of soloists singing together, such as the vocal quartet in bars 62–77 of *NAM 29* (pages 303–304). You should be able to distinguish between all these different vocal groups. Note that the term **a cappella** is used to indicate a vocal piece performed without accompaniment (as in *NAM 30*).

Texture

Texture is one of the most misunderstood words in music exams. It refers to the simultaneous layers in a piece of music (such as treble and bass, or melody and accompaniment) and the way they relate to each other. Aim to become familiar with the terms below – try to understand them thoroughly as you are unlikely to get marks for identifying texture with vague descriptions such as 'thin' or 'rich'.

Monophony. A texture that consists of a single unaccompanied melody, such as the music of *NAM 61* (page 530). An unaccompanied melody performed in **octaves** (e.g. bars 20–22 of *NAM 24* on page 260) is a type of monophonic texture, as is an unaccompanied melody performed by a number of people in **unison** (e.g. bars 3–4 of *NAM 32* on page 344).

Heterophony. A texture in which a melody and a decorated version of the same melody are heard simultaneously, as in bars 9–15 of *NAM 29* (page 300) where the orchestra play a decorated version of the choral melody that occurs in these same bars.

Homophony. A texture in which one of the parts (often the highest) has the main melody, while the others accompany. The last five bars of *NAM 30* on page 306 of the *New Anthology* are homophonic – the voices all move together in a purely chordal style and the top part forms the main melody.

Melody and accompaniment. This is also a homophonic texture (because just one part has the melody) but it is one in which the accompaniment usually has some independence. *NAM 39* (page 363) shows an example in which the piano accompaniment is based on repeated chords. In *NAM 17* you can hear accompaniment figures based on broken chords (viola, bar 19–28, page 209), on arpeggios (cello, bars 29–36, page 210), and on syncopated chords (violin and viola, bars 29–36). The Alberti bass is a particular type of broken-chord figuration in which the notes of a chord appear in the order low, high, middle and high again. Named after an Italian who was one of the first composers to make frequent use of the device, an Alberti bass can be heard in *NAM 22*, bars 71–80 (left hand) on page 255 of the *New Anthology*.

Counterpoint. Music that consists of two or more melodies with independent rhythms is said to have a contrapuntal texture. For example, *NAM 15* (page 200) consists of a three simultaneous melodic lines, two for violins and one for the violone (notice that an organ also plays the chords indicated by figures in the continuo part). The term 'counterpoint' is now often used interchangeably with **polyphony**, although it is more common to use polyphony when referring to vocal music of the renaissance.

Antiphony. A texture in which groups of singers and/or instruments are heard performing alternately. The groups are often widely separated, e.g. by being in different parts of a large church. You can hear antiphonal textures in the recording of *NAM 14* (page 194) and on **track 27** of **Aural Matters in Practice**.

You may also be asked to state whether a passage of music you hear is in two, three or four parts. The number of parts is not necessarily the same as the number of instruments. For instance, *NAM 22* (page 253) starts with a two-part texture, even though it is played on just one instrument, the piano.

In *NAM 7* page 151 begins with oboes and horns, first in a two-part texture, then in a three-part texture (from bar 36) and finally in a four-part texture (bars 41–42). In *NAM 32*, after the monophonic start on page 344 you can hear two-part vocal textures (bars 2, 5 and 6) and then a four-part vocal texture in bars 7–10 on page 345. Bars 22–29 of *NAM 30* (starting on page 305) consist of a three-part vocal texture.

Here are some other terms that are often used when discussing texture.

Dialogue is a texture in which a musical idea passes from one part to another. In bars 61–65 of *NAM 17* (starting on page 212) there is dialogue between the first violin and the clarinet and bassoon.

A **counter-melody** is a tune that fits in counterpoint with another melody. At bar 55 in *NAM 9* (page 164) a counter-melody is played on the first violin above a theme played on the second violin. A related device is the **descant** – a counter-melody performed above the melody of a hymn tune. There is a trumpet descant in verse 2 of the hymn on **CD1 track 7** of the accompanying CDs – starting at 1'41" into the track.

Doubling refers to the simultaneous performance of the same melody, either in unison or octaves. In the first eight bars of *NAM 2* (page 31) the bassoons double the cellos in unison, while the oboes double the violins an octave higher (with some rhythmic simplications).

Tutti refers to a texture in which the full forces of an ensemble are employed. *Tutti* sections often contrast with passages for a soloist, or for reduced forces. For instance, in *NAM 1* just a solo violin with light accompaniment is heard in bars 83–88 (page 8) followed by a *tutti* entry in bar 89.

An **ostinato** is a melodic or rhythmic pattern that is repeated throughout a passage of music – as in the four-note ostinato for timpani, pianos and harp that starts in bar 163 of *NAM 31* (page 337). A **ground bass** is a type of ostinato – 'When I am laid in earth' (*NAM* pages 356–358) is built on a four-bar ground.

A **pedal** is a sustained or repeated note against which changing harmonies are heard. *NAM 16* contains a pedal on the dominant in bars 16–28 (page 202) and a tonic pedal in bars 107–111 (page 205).

The following features are often found in contrapuntal textures:

Canon. A device in which a melody in one part fits with the same melody in a different part starting a few beats later. The type of song known as a round is a canon that continually repeats. You can hear a series of canons between the trumpet and oboe in the first movement of *NAM 28* (pages 288–295).

Imitation. A device in which a melodic idea in one part is copied immediately by another part while the first part continues. Unlike canon, only the opening contour of the original idea needs to be repeated in an imitative part, and the imitation does not have to be exact: see bars 56–64 of *NAM 26* (pages 268–269) where each voice enters in imitation on the word *aeternae*.

Fugue. A fugue is a contrapuntal composition that begins with a melody (called the subject) which is introduced by each part in turn. As each new part announces the subject the previous part continues with a new melody called the countersubject. In the fugue of *NAM 25* (page 263) notice how the subject begins on the tonic (A) but when the same melody enters in the left hand at bar 5, it is transposed to start on the dominant (E). This alternation of tonic- and dominant-based entries is characteristic of the start of a fugue, and can be heard in the more complex fugal texture illustrated in *Aural Matters*, page 108.

Finally, when describing timbre and texture, try to be as precise as possible. For instance, in *NAM 1* you could observe that the flutes play in thirds in bars 4–6, but in sixths in bars 9–12. Or you could note that an important aspect of *NAM 9* (page 163) is that all four string parts are written in a low tessitura, helping to give the movement its dark quality. And if you are asked to name an instrument, try to give its *exact* name (e.g. 'trombone') rather than just saying 'brass'.

Excerpt A

Listen TWICE to the first 41 seconds of *CD2 track 1*

(a) This music is for brass ensemble. How many instruments are there in the ensemble? *4* **(1)**

(b) They are all the same type of brass instrument. What type is it? *[handwritten]* **(1)**

(c) The first section lasts for 13 seconds. Describe the texture of this section. *monophonic* **(1)**

(d) Describe the texture of the remainder of the extract. *Polyphonic* **(1)**

(e) Which of the following is heard at the start of the second section? Underline your answer.

descant   antiphony   dialogue   imitation   <u>canon</u>   **(1)**

> In this type of question you must make sure that you underline only **one** answer. You will not get a mark if you underline two or more answers, even if one of them is correct.

Excerpt B

Listen TWICE to the first 70 seconds of *CD2 track 6*

(f) Name **two** instruments heard in this extract. .... and .... **(2)**

(g) Underline **two** terms below that best describe the vocal part:

melismatic   syllabic   glissando   sprechgesang   recitative   **(2)**

Total: 9 marks

Excerpt A

Listen TWICE to *CD1 track 18*

(a) Name the only instrument heard playing in this carol. .... **(1)**

(b) This carol has two verses. What type of voice sings the first verse? .... **(1)**

(c) Describe the texture of the first verse. .... **(1)**

(d) Verse two is sung by a choir. How many voice parts are there in this choir? .... **(1)**

(e) Complete the following sentence.

At the start of verse 2 the choir sings alternately in .... and in .... **(2)**

Excerpt B

Listen to *CD1 track 19* (the music is played twice on this track)

(f) What type of instruments are heard in this extract? .... **(1)**

(g) Which of the following describes this type of ensemble. Underline **one** answer.

duet   trio   quartet   wind band   military band   jazz band   **(1)**

(h) Describe the texture of this music as accurately as possible. .... **(1)**

> Spaces are usually designed for the length of answer expected – don't write too much!

Total: 9 marks

Test 3

Excerpt A

Listen TWICE to the first 82 seconds of *CD2 track 11*

(a) Which of the following best describes the texture heard at the start of the introduction to this song? Underline **one** answer.

unison **octaves** **homophonic** **antiphonal** **contrapuntal** Polyphonic **(1)**

(b) What type of voice sings the solo? ...Tenor... **(1)**

(c) Complete the missing terms in the following sentences.

After the introduction the texture throughout the rest of the extract could be described as ...homophonic... ✓ . The pianist plays chords but also ~~...~~ copy / mirror ✓ the singer, often in ...unison... ✓ as well as at the octave above. **(3)**

Excerpt B

Listen TWICE to the first 30 seconds of *CD1 track 12*

(d) Name the texture heard at the very start (and again at the end) of this extract. .... **(1)**

(e) Name the following instruments heard in this septet:

(i) The only brass instrument .... **(1)**

(ii) Either one of the two woodwind instruments .... **(1)**

(iii) The lowest-sounding of the four string instruments .... **(1)**

Total: 9 marks

Test 4

Excerpt A

Listen TWICE to the first 40 seconds of *CD1 track 5*

(a) Complete the missing terms in the following description of this excerpt.

At the start two instruments play .... with the piano. One is a violin and the other is a .... They use a playing technique called .... and play the same notes a(n) .... apart. A different playing technique used later by these instruments is called .... This type of chamber-music ensemble is called a .... **(6)**

Excerpt B

Listen TWICE to the first 40 seconds of *CD1 track 6*

(b) Describe as accurately as possible the type of choir singing this music. .... **(1)**

(c) Which of the following best describes the musical texture? Underline **one** answer.

imitative homophonic heterophonic monophonic fugal **(1)**

(d) This music is performed *a capella*. What does that mean? .... **(1)**

Total: 9 marks

Excerpt A   Listen TWICE to the first 75 seconds of *CD1 track 2*

(a) Describe the timbres and textures in the first section of the music by completing the three missing words in the following account.

The extract starts with a melody played on a(n) .... This melody is

immediately .... by a violin. These two soloists are accompanied by

a group of instruments known as the ....   **(3)**

(b) Two singers are featured in the second part of the extract.
One has a bass voice. What type of voice does the other singer have? .... **(1)**

(c) State precisely how the part sung by the bass relates to the part sung by the other singer.

....   **(2)**

Excerpt B   Listen TWICE to the first 30 seconds of *CD2 track 9*

(d) The lower of the two voices is a tenor. What is the higher voice in this duet? .... **(1)**

(e) What is the relationship between the voices in the first phrase? .... **(1)**

(f) Just before the end of the excerpt the two voices sing separately. Which of the following best describes their relationship at this point? Tick your chosen answer.

☐ The tenor imitates the higher voice.
☐ The tenor doubles the higher voice.
☐ The tenor echoes the higher voice an octave lower.
☐ The tenor echoes the higher voice a 10th lower.   **(1)**

Total: 9 marks

Excerpt A   Listen TWICE to the whole of *CD1 track 3*

(a) Describe the musical resoruces and textures heard in this piece.

> If you are faced with an 'open' question like this you can answer in note form or in sentences. To help keep you focused on the question, we have given approximate CD timings for each main change of texture. Try to make at least one point about each of these locations.

0:01 ....

0:18 ....

0:54 ....

1:27 ....

1:57 ....   **(5)**

[10]

Excerpt B   Listen TWICE to the first 62 seconds of *CD1 track 21*

(b) Underline the type of male voice singing this song.

       treble   male alto   counter-tenor   tenor   baritone   bass   **(1)**

(c) Complete the following sentences.

The excerpt consists of a verse and a chorus. In the verse the word-setting is entirely syllabic

but in the chorus it is entirely .... The type of singing in the chorus is

called vocalising because ....

The singer's melody moves almost entirely by step, whereas the texture of the piano

accompaniment consists entirely of a bass part and ....   **(3)**

                                                        Total: 9 marks

Test 7

Excerpt A   Listen TWICE to the first 88 seconds of *CD1 track 20*

(a) Complete the following sentence:
This music is written for six instruments – a solo violin, piano and a .... quartet. **(1)**

(b) In the first section, which is 43 seconds long, the solo violin plays the melody.
Briefly describe the accompaniment played by:

    (i)   the piano ....   **(1)**

    (ii) the lower instruments in the quartet ....   **(1)**

(c) A second section, marked by a modulation to a major key, starts after 43 seconds.
Explain how the texture described in question (b) changes in this second section.

....

....

....   **(2)**

(d) Name the instrument that plays a counter-melody to the piano melody in the last few bars of

the excerpt. ....   **(1)**

Excerpt B   Listen TWICE to *CD1 track 27*

(e) After a four-note monophonic introduction, this piece maintains the same texture throughout.

How many voice parts are there in this texture? ....   **(1)**

(f) What do you notice about the relationship of the two highest parts?

....

....   **(2)**

                                                        Total: 9 marks

Excerpt A   Listen TWICE to the first 52 seconds of *CD1 track 15*

(a) Which of the following describes the opening texture of this extract? Underline your answer.

      unison   <u>two-part</u>   three-part   four-part   (1)

(b) Name the instrument that plays the melody in this opening section. ...Viola.... (1)

(c) The next section is louder and in a major key. Mention **one** way in which the composer
    thickens the texture in this section.

    ....By adding more instruments.............. (1)

(d) Underline **two** features of the bass part in the final section.

      arco   tremolo   <u>pizzicato</u>   col legno

      dominant pedal   <u>muted</u>   glissando   (2)

(e) What type of ensemble have you heard in this extract? Underline your answer.

      string orchestra   string trio   <u>string quartet</u> ✗   string quintet   (1)

Excerpt B   3/6   Listen TWICE to the first 30 seconds of *CD1 track 22*

(f) Using words from the following list, complete the sentence below.

      canon   ostinato   antiphony   tremolo   flutter-tonguing   vibrato   glissando

    Throughout the extract the flautist uses ...flutter tonguing... ✗... and the pianist plays
    a(n) ...ostinato... ✓ . In each of the first two phrases a short ...glissando... ✓
    can be heard between the highest notes in the flute part.   (3)

            2/3   **Total: 9 marks**

Excerpt A   Listen TWICE to the first 37 seconds of *CD2 track 10*

(a) What is the relationship between the two upper parts of the choir?

    ...Harmonised in 3rds and 6ths... ✓   (1)

(b) How do the two lower parts of the choral texture relate to the two upper parts?

    ...Harmonised in 5ths x 8ves...   (1)

(c) What term describes the style of these choral parts? ...Antiphonal... ✗   (1)

(d) What is the role of the piano accompaniment in the introduction?

    ...Provide a dominant pedal...   (1)

(e) Identify the type of voice of the solo singer. ...Tenor...   (1)

(f) How does the piano accompaniment change when the soloist enters?

    ...The piano plays ... the ostinato but is added upper notes... (1)
    & added bassline

Excerpt B

(g) Describe the texture at the start of this extract. ....*Monophonic*............*Sus*............ ~~²/₂~~ **(1)**

(h) Briefly describe the texture of the passage starting at 0'35" leading into the entry of the piano.
..................*Homophonic*......*Texture*....*Melody in 3rds*....~~and Strings~~...... **(1)**

(i) When the pianist plays the melody from the start of the extract, how has the texture changed?
..........*The Strings provide accompaniment* ~~to~~ *Homophonic*......... ~~(1)~~

Total: 9 marks

6/9

2. Comparison of Performances

This is the second question on the AS Listening Paper. You will hear two different performances of the same music, for which no notation will be provided. You will hear the performances alternately, **three** times in all, in the order A–B–A–B–A–B. You will be asked to identify the differences between the two performances in areas such as tempo, dynamics, ornamentation and instrumentation. You may also be asked to express and justify an opinion about the performances. You will not be asked about the similarities between the two versions.

Since the compact discs accompanying this book include only one performance of each item, you will need access to some additional recordings in order to work through the exercises in this chapter. As far as possible we have chosen examples that are likely to be available in libraries, that are often broadcast on the radio and that are available on bargain-price CDs. In some cases, short free samples of recordings may also be available on the world-wide web. You may not be able to find all of these recordings, but you should find that you can adapt the style of questions to other pieces. For instance, CD libraries often include several different performances of famous works such as Beethoven's symphonies, Vivaldi's violin concertos known as *The Four Seasons* and Bach's orchestral suites. Listening to the same short passage from two different recordings of works such as these will help give you further practice. Also look out for different performances of the works in *NAM* – for instance, there are dozens of different recordings of *NAM 1* available, one of which you could compare with the performance on the anthology CD.

In the exam there are likely to be 4–6 questions that require a single-word or very short answer, plus one or two that will require you to write or complete a short commentary. It is important to remember that you will not get marks for anything in your commentary that merely repeats information from earlier questions on the same music. In particular you should be careful not to fall into the trap of repeating statements that have appeared in 'true or false' questions, as some of these *will* be incorrect. Sneak a look over the page and note that in question (b) you are asked to name an instrument that is heard only in Performance B. Even if you get this right there would be no point in repeating this information in question (e) since you will not get any more marks for making the same point again.

There is not a lot of extra terminology to learn for this question, although you should of course know that **tempo** refers to the speed of music, and **dynamics** to its relative loudness and quietness. So examiners may expect you to spot that one performance contains a *crescendo* at the point where the dynamics remain unchanged in the other. You may also need to comment on differences in ornamentation or rhythm – for instance, a jazz version of the music might be played with swung rhythm where the original version has straight rhythm. The main types of ornament you are likely to encounter are:

- The **acciaccatura** (♪). A very short note played with or immediately before the main note, and usually one step above or below it.
- The **mordent** (᷉). A rapid movement from the main note to a note a step away, and back again.
- The **trill** (*tr*). A rapid alternation of two notes a step apart.
- The **turn** (∾). A four-note pattern that starts one step above the main note, falls to the main note, falls again to the step below and ends by rising to the main note.

We will consider a few further matters of terminology as we work through the rest of this chapter.

This test is based on a comparison of **CD1 track 19** with the recording of the same music on **CD1 track 29** of *Rule Brittania*, a low-price double CD from Nimbus (NI 7067/8) that also contains a version of 'Rule Brittania' that you could use for test 11. Alternatively you could compare **CD1 track 19** with the recording of this work by the Oxford Camerata that appears on several budget-priced compilations from Naxos, including *Purcell: Music on the Death of Queen Mary* (8.553129). See also the introduction to test 12.

We will call the version on **CD1 track 19** 'Performance A' and the other version 'Performance B'.

Listen to your two chosen recordings **three** times each, in the order A–B–A–B–A–B, as you answer the following questions.

(a) Underline **two** statements below that are TRUE.

Performance A is played by brass and woodwind instruments alone.

Performance A is played by brass instruments alone.

Performance B includes one or more woodwind instruments.

Performance B includes one or more string instruments.

Performance B includes one or more percussion instruments. **(2)**

(b) Name an instrument that is heard only in Performance B. .... **(2)**

(c) What is the difference in pitch between the two performances?

.... **(2)**

(d) Compare the tempo of the two versions.

.... **(1)**

(e) Briefly comment on any other notable differences you hear between the two performances.

....

....

....

.... **(4)**

(f) This music was written by Henry Purcell for the funeral procession to Westminster Abbey of the body of Queen Mary in 1695. Explain which performance you consider to be the more effective in portraying this occasion, being careful to justify your choice. ◄

> In questions like this you will not get a mark for merely saying that you like performance A more than B (or vice versa). You will have to say *why* you think that one performance fulfils the intended purpose more successfully than the other.

....

.... **(1)**

Total: 12 marks

This test is based on a comparison of the song 'Rule, Brittania' on **CD2 track 23** with the arrangement of the same music by Sir Malcolm Sargent on **track 19** of *The Best of the Proms*, a mid-price CD from EMI (566593-2). There are many others recordings of the Sargent arrangement, which can also often be heard on television and radio in the BBC's broadcasts of the last night of the proms each September.

We will call the first 56 seconds of **CD2 track 23** 'Performance A' and we will use 'Performance B' to refer to the first 1 minute and 40 seconds of the other version.

Both versions contain the following three sections of music:

An instrumental introduction
The first verse of the song sung by a solo voice
A refrain sung to the words *Rule, Brittania, Brittania rule the waves; Britons never will be slaves.*

Listen to the recordings **three** times each, in the order A–B–A–B–A–B, as you answer the following questions.

(a) (i)   Name the type of voice singing the solo in Performance A.   ....   **(1)**

(ii)   Name the type of voice singing the solo in Performance B.   ....   **(1)**

(iii)   Which of the two singers adopts a more *legato* approach, A or B?   ....   **(1)**

(b) Suggest **two** reasons why Performance B takes almost twice as long as Performance A.

(i)   ....   **(1)**

(ii)   ....   **(1)**

(c) What is the difference in pitch between the two performances?

....   **(2)**

(d) Using phrases from the list below, complete the sentence that follows.

> **wind band**   **symphony orchestra**   **string orchestra**
> **big band**   **chamber orchestra**   **brass ensemble**

The accompaniment in Performance A is given by a .... whose

members play period instruments. In Performance B the accompaniment is played by a

.... whose members play modern instruments.   **(2)**

(e) (i)   Name an instrument heard only in Performance A.   ....   **(1)**

(ii)   Name an instrument heard only in Performance B.   ....   **(1)**

(f) Briefly comment on **one** other difference you hear between the two performances.

....

....   **(1)**

Total: 12 marks

[15]

This test is based on a comparison of the first 32 seconds of 'Sound the Trumpet' on **CD1 track 14** with the performance of the same extract on *Odes for Queen Mary*, a low-priced CD from Virgin (VM 561844-2). There are many other good recordings that could be used instead of the second one mentioned here, including those on *Purcell: Complete Odes and Welcome Songs, Volume 8* (Hyperion CDA66598, full price) and *Purcell: Odes for St Cecilia's Day / Music for Queen Mary* (Veritas Twofers, 561582-2, bargain-price double CD). The latter also includes a performance of the music for Test 10.

We will call the extract from **CD2 track 23** 'Performance A' and we will call the extract from the other recording 'Performance B'.

Listen to the recordings **three** times each, in the order A–B–A–B–A–B, as you answer the following questions.

(a) Complete the missing words in the following account.

Performance A is sung by two .... voices and is accompanied on the ....

Performance B is sung by two .... voices and is accompanied by a continuo

group consisting of a(n) .... and a(n) ....   **(5)**

(b) What is the difference in pitch between the two performances?

.... **(2)**

> We have encountered this type of question before. Why is the same piece sometimes performed in a different key? It could be to make the music easier to play, but this is unlikley to be a reason for professional performers. One more likely explanation is that a song may be performed at a different pitch to suit better the range of a particular singer. Another explanation is that music from the 18th century and earlier is sometimes performed at a different (usually lower) pitch than notated in order to recreate the way it might have sounded when it was composed. This is because it is believed that several centuries ago pitch standards were at least a semitone lower than today. Both of these points apply to our present comparison, since neither is in the key in which the music was notated by its composer.

(c) Mention **three** ways (other than instrumentation) in which the accompaniment of Performance A differs from the accompaniment of Performance B.

....

....

.... **(3)**

(d) This piece was composed in 1694. Which **two** aspects of performance A lead you to think that it must be a modern arrangement of the original music heard in performance B?

....

.... **(2)**

Total: 12 marks

This test is based on a comparison of the recording of *La Réjouissance* from Handel's 'Music for the Royal Fireworks' on **CD1 track 1** with the recording of the same movement on **track 5** of *Baroque Suites and Concertos*, a bargain-price CD from Decca Eloquence (467 415-2). The latter version, which is from a recording by Sir Neville Marriner and the Academy of St Martin-in-the-Fields, can also be found on a number of other compilations of baroque music.

In both versions you will hear two sections of music, each of which is repeated. You will need to listen to the first 75 seconds of **CD1 track 1**, which we will call 'Performance A', and the first 86 seconds of the other version, which we will call 'Performance B'.

Listen to the excerpts **three** times each, in the order A–B–A–B–A–B, as you answer the following questions.

(a) Which performance is taken at the slower tempo, A or B? .... **(1)**

(b) Performance A is in the key of D♭ major. In what key is Performance B? .... **(2)**

(c) Complete the **four** blank boxes in the following table to show how the instrumentation of the main melodic material differs between the two performances:

	Performance A	Performance B
First half	Trumpets	Trumpets
Repeat of first half		
Second half		
Repeat of second half	(same as in the repeat of the first half)	Trumpets

(4)

(d) (i) Name a percussion instrument heard only in Performance A. .... **(1)**

(ii) Name a keyboard instrument heard only in Performance B. .... **(1)**

(e) Identify **one** other difference between the two performances.

....

.... **(1)**

(f) This music was written for outdoor performance at a fireworks festival. Which performance do you think is more effective in portraying this occasion? Give **two** reasons to justify your choice.

....

.... **(2)**

Total: 12 marks

[17]

This test is based on a comparison of **CD2 track 8** with a performance of the same movement on *Bach's Goldberg Variations*, a CD from Telarc (CD83479).

We will call the extract from **CD2 track 8** 'Performance A' and we will call the extract from the other recording 'Performance B'. The music consists of the following sections:

Performance A	Performance B
	Short introduction
Section 1, which is repeated	Section 1 (not repeated)
Section 2, which is repeated	Section 2 (not repeated)
	Variation of Sections 1 and 2

Listen to the recordings **three** times each, in the order A–B–A–B–A–B, as you answer the questions. Note that this test is a little longer than those you are likely to be set in an examination.

(a) Which performance is taken at the faster tempo, A or B? .... **(1)**

(b) Which of the following statements is true? Tick your chosen answer.

☐ Performance A is approximately a tone lower than Performance B.

☐ Performance A is approximately a semitone higher than Performance B.

☐ The two performances are at approximately the same pitch. **(1)**

(c) Name **two** instruments that are heard only in Performance B and briefly state how each is played.

Instrument: .... It is played ....

Instrument: .... It is played .... **(4)**

(d) Describe the main differences between the two performances, apart from any differences in structure, speed, pitch and instrumentation that have already been mentioned.

....

....

....

....

....

.... **(6)**

Total: 12 marks

The group that recorded Performance B have also recorded an arrangement of Handel's *La Réjouissance* which could be compared with **CD1 track 1** (see Test 13). It can be found on track 13 of *Handel: Water Music and Royal Fireworks*, Telarc CD83544.

3. Aural Recognition

After one minute for reading the questions an excerpt of music will be played five times. There will be a skeleton score of at least part of the passage. You must answer *either* **Option A**, which entails adding notation to the score (rhythms and pitches, and possibly chords) *or* **Option B**, which requires you to answer questions about the music's context (where and when it might have been written, the type of work from which it comes, its style, its purpose, how it expresses any text that may be sung, and so forth).

Option A

The advantage of choosing this option is that it is the best possible preparation for Question 4, but you will almost certainly need to work through a number of graded exercises in pitch and rhythm dictation. Some material to help can be found in the chapter on melody dictation in *Aural Matters*. Try to exercise your perception of pitch and rhythm for a few minutes every day. Here are a couple of suggestions.

Pitch

Most simple melodies are based on moving stepwise (conjunct motion) and moving up and down the notes of triads (usually chords I, IV and V). These will be easy to identify if you practise singing fragments of scales and broken chord patterns. See how many different permutations you can invent, but remember that it is essential always to know which note in the scale you are singing, so either sing the number of the scale step (as shown below) or sing the patterns to tonic solf-fa ('doh ray me' etc.) if you prefer:

1 2 3 4 5   5 6 5 4 3   2 1 sev-en 1   1 3 5 3 8 5   *etc.*

Remember to practise minor scales as well, and as you become more confident try to include broken chords based on triads IV and V, and try patterns that omit some scale steps (e.g. 1–3–4–5).

Rhythm

Try inventing rhythm patterns that combine easily confused rhythms, such as dotted patterns. You could practise these to nonsense syllables, as shown in the first pattern below, or you could combine rhythm practice with scale and triad training:

Dum dumm-da tum-ti dum   1 5 1 3 5   4 3 2 1 7 6   5   *etc.*

Again, as you become more confident extend your practice to include other rhythm patterns such as triplets, compound-time groupings (e.g. ♫♫ ♫ ♪♫ | ♩ ♪♩. |) and tied-note patterns (e.g. ♩ ♫♫♫ ♫♫ :||).

When practising the tests, note that in questions in which you are required to add pitches to a given rhythm you **must** include that rhythm in your answer and not just write note-heads without stems.

To help you follow the music we have included CD timings in grey boxes in the scores of the first three tests. For instance, 1'05" refers to one minute and five seconds from the start of the relevant CD track. Note that actual exam papers do not include CD timings.

Option B

If you choose this option you are likely to have to identify various features of the music, including the style, period and possibly the type of work, and to give reasons for your identification. You will find that, with the exception of basic terminology covered in GCSE Music, we have exemplified most of the terms you need to know for this option on pages 47–59 (where they are printed **bold**). You should read those pages and listen to all the examples before working through this chapter. The six tests in this chapter also cover many of the most of the important terms (again printed **bold**). Since this is not a dictionary we have not attempted to define all of them, so if you come across a term you don't understand you should ask your teacher to explain and illustrate it with appropriate music.

Listen **FIVE TIMES** to the first 42 seconds of *CD 2, Track 17*   Answer *either* Option A *or* Option B

Option A. On the skeleton score printed below and opposite add musical notation as directed.
Option B. Answer the following questions about the music. You may refer to the score if you wish.

(a) Underline the type of voice singing this song:

   counter-tenor   tenor   baritone   bass   **(1)**

(b) Underline the type of vocal music from which this extract is taken:

   aria   madrigal   air   Lied   recitative   **(1)**

(c) How does the opening relate to the singer's first phrase? .... **(1)**

(d) In addition to bowed string instruments, what
   other instrument can you hear in the accompaniment? .... **(1)**

(e) The music begins in a major key. Underline the key to which it modulates:

   the tonic minor   the dominant   the relative minor   **(1)**

(f) Name the **three** chords used most frequently in this extract. .... **(3)**

(g) Look back at your answers to questions (c), (d) and (e) then suggest:

   (i)   a year in which this music might have been composed: .... **(1)**

   (ii) the type of work in which it might have been performed: .... **(1)**

(h) In what type of venue might the first performance of this song have been heard?

   .... **(2)**

ADD PITCHES OF MELODY **(2)**

ADD RHYTHM TO THESE PITCHES **(5)**

[20]

ADD THE VOCAL MELODY (3)

ADD THE PITCHES OF THE BASS PART (2)

Total: 12 marks

[21]

Listen **FIVE TIMES** to the first 75 seconds of *CD 1, Track 13*   Answer *either* Option A *or* Option B

Option A. On the skeleton score printed below and opposite add musical notation as directed.
Option B. Answer the following questions about the music. You may refer to the score if you wish.

(a) Name the wind instruments and describe their role in the whole extract:

    (i)   Wind instruments .... **(1)**

    (ii) Role of wind instruments ....

              ....

              .... **(3)**

(b) Name the bass instrument and describe the music it plays in the first two bars.

    (i)   Bass instrument .... **(1)**

    (ii) Part played in the first two bars ....

              .... **(3)**

(c) Name the *other* continuo instrument. .... **(1)**

(d) This music comes from a composition that contains recitatives, arias and a choral ensemble accompanied by a chamber orchestra. Underline the term below which you think most accurately describes this type of work.

        Sonata   **Cantata**   **Lied**   **Motet**   **Anthem** **(1)**

(e) In which of the following musical periods was this written? Underline your answer.

        Renaissance   **Baroque**   **Classical**   **Romantic**   **20th-century** **(1)**

(f) Suggest the name of a likely composer. .... **(1)**

ADD PITCHES OF MELODY **(3)**

Soprano: Scha - fe __ kön - nen

si - cher wei - den __ wo ein __ gu - ter Hir - te __ wacht,

0:26

ADD RHYTHM OF PLUCKED
STRING INSTRUMENT

rhythm of treble instruments:

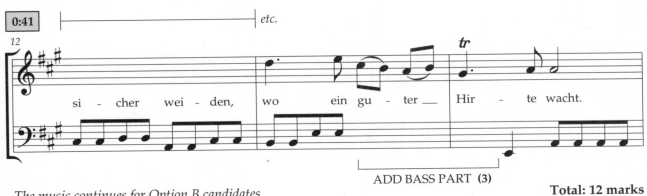

Scha - fe __ kön - nen __ si - cher wei - den __ Scha - fe __ kön - nen __

(3)

ADD RHYTHM OF TREBLE INSTRUMENTS **(3)**

0:41 ──────────── *etc.*

si - cher wei - den, wo ein gu - ter __ Hir - te wacht.

ADD BASS PART **(3)**

The music continues for Option B candidates

Total: 12 marks

Listen **FIVE TIMES** to the first 55 seconds of *CD 2, Track 2*   Answer *either* Option A *or* Option B

Option A. On the skeleton score printed opposite add musical notation as directed.
Option B. Answer the following questions about the music. You may refer to the score if you wish.

(a) Name the **two** instruments that provide a 'harmonic filling' between treble and bass.

(i) .... (ii) .... **(2)**

(b) Name two ways in which the repeat of the first section differs from the first time it is played.

(i) ....

(ii) .... **(2)**

(c) Describe the chord heard at the end of every one of the four sections of this piece.

.... **(2)**

(d) Describe the type of rhythm played by the violinist throughout most of the last two sections.

.... **(1)**

(e) Which one of the following best describes the scale patterns heard in the bass?
Underline your answer.

chromatic   harmonic minor   melodic minor

pentatonic   major **(1)**

(f) Underline **one** term which best describes the bass part of the whole excerpt.

sequence   ground   obbligato   ostinato   accompaniment **(1)**

(g) Underline **two** terms that best describe the whole excerpt.

march   dance   procession   concerto

fugue   variations   canon   minuet **(2)**

(h) Underline the century in which you think this music was composed.

17th   18th   19th   20th **(1)**

Don't forget the note about 'centuries' on page 47. For instance, if you think this piece was composed in about 1850 the answer would be 19th century – not 18th century.

(The music is performed a semitone higher than printed)

Total: 12 marks

Listen **FIVE TIMES** to the first 45 seconds of *CD 2, Track 21*   Answer *either* Option A *or* Option B

Option A. On the skeleton score printed below and opposite add musical notation as directed.
Option B. Answer the following questions about the music. You may refer to the score if you wish.

(a) Choose appropriate terms from the following list to complete the sentence printed below:

   chordal   homophonic   monophonic   melody-and-accompaniment   two-part

   There is a .... texture in the piano introduction, but the vocal and piano

   parts together make a .... texture.   **(2)**

(b) Underline the word that best describes the type of voice singing this extract:

   counter-tenor   tenor   baritone   bass   **(1)**

(c) Underline the word that most accurately describes the type of vocal music from which this
   extract is taken:

   aria   ayre   Lied   madrigal   recitative   **(1)**

(d) The composition is entitled 'May Song'. State **three** ways in which the music suggests the
   poet's simple joy in the beauty of springtime.

   ....

   ....   **(3)**

(e) Where might a song of this sort have been performed in the period when it was first composed?
   Underline your choice of venue:

   concert hall   church   home   theatre   **(1)**

(f) Suggest a likely composer .... and year of composition: .... **(2)**

(g) Justify your answers to question (f) by commenting briefly on the phrase structure of the vocal
   part and the harmony of the whole song.

   ....

   ....   **(2)**

Listen **FIVE TIMES** to the first 40 seconds of *CD 2, Track 5*   Answer *either* Option A *or* Option B

Option A. On the skeleton score printed below and opposite add musical notation as directed.
Option B. Answer the following questions about the music. You may refer to the score if you wish.

(a) The following five questions refer to the orchestral introduction.

   (i)   The opening is played *tutti*. What does this mean? .... **(1)**

   (ii) Describe the texture of the loud music at the start. .... **(1)**

   (iii) Name the brass instrument that plays a sustained note. .... **(1)**

   (iv) Name the woodwind instrument that plays a melodic solo. .... **(1)**

   (v)   Name the two sections of the orchestra that play antiphonally with each other:

      .... and .... **(2)**

(b) Chose appropriate words or phrases from this list to complete the sentence below:

   fourths and fifths   **thirds and sixths**   **octaves**   **unison**

   The tenors and basses sing in .... and the sopranos and altos sing

   in .... **(2)**

(c) Underline **two** of the following words or phrases that most accurately describe the setting of the text printed at the foot of the opposite page.

   call and response   **verse and chorus**   **strophic**   **through-composed** **(2)**

(d) Underline the year in which you think this music was first performed:

   1796   **1846**   **1896**   **1946**   **1996** **(1)**

(e) From which of the vocal genres listed below might this extract have been taken?
   Think about your answer to question (d) before underlining **one** of the following words:

   cantata   **musical**   **opera**   **operetta**   **oratorio** **(1)**

The text continues: Mounts the golden Sun God high,
                      Shaded from his fury heated
                      Still at tea you find us seated.

Total: 12 marks

Answer *either* Option A *or* Option B

Option A. Listen **FIVE TIMES** to the first 66 seconds of *CD 1, Track 14*.
On the skeleton score printed on pages 31–33 add musical notation as directed.

Option B. Listen **FIVE TIMES** to all of *CD 1, Track 14*.
Answer the following questions about the music.
You may refer to the score if you wish but note that many of the questions refer to the second section of the extract, for which only the words are given in the score.

(a) For each part of this question, select words from the following lists to complete the sentences that follow:

   (i) **chromatic**   **syllabic**   **modal**   **melismatic**

      The setting of the word *trumpet* in the first section is .... whereas

      the setting of the word *glories* at the end of the song is ....   **(2)**

   (ii) **echoes**   **imitates**   **inverts**

      The accompaniment .... the vocal repetitions of the word *sound*.   **(1)**

   (iii) **triadic**   **sequential**   **conjunct**

      echoes   **imitates**   **invert**s

      The first tenor's melody for *All the instruments of joy* is .... and

      the second tenor .... this melody.   **(2)**

(b) This song comes from a piece written to celebrate the birthday of a British monarch. What does the composer do to ensure that the words *to celebrate* will be clearly heard?

.... **(2)**

(c) The song is based on a ground heard in the bass during the introduction. How does the composer change this ground in the second section?

.... **(1)**

(d) Which **two** musical features suggest that the original version of this song was composed by Henry Purcell at the end of the 17th century, *and* which **two** features suggest that the version heard here was arranged by Benjamin Britten in the middle of the last century?

Purcell because:

(i) ....

(ii) ....

and Britten because:

(iii) ....

(iv) .... **(4)**

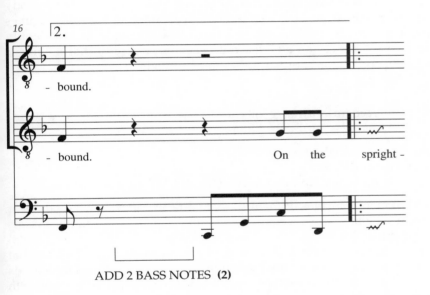

ADD 2 BASS NOTES **(2)**

For Option B candidates, the second section continues with the following words
(*sprightly* means lively, *Oboy* is an old spelling of oboe, and *numbers* means groups of notes):

> On the sprightly Oboy play.
> All the instruments of joy,
>   That skilful numbers can employ
> To celebrate the glories of this day.

Like the first section, the second section is repeated.

Total: 12 marks

4. Perception of Tonality and Harmony

An excerpt of music will be played four times and you will be asked questions about the tonality and harmony of the music. Before you hear the music for the first time you will be given two minutes to read the questions and to look through the single-stave skeleton score that will be provided.

Tonality

You will be tested on your ability to identify key relationships. These could include:

- modulations from the tonic to the dominant
- modulations from the tonic to the relative minor (or relative major for music starting in a minor key),
- passages which change from tonic major to tonic minor (or *vice versa*).

You will not be asked to name specific keys (such as G major or E minor). In practice, however, you might well find it easier to think in specific keys. So if the music starts in G and you are asked to describe the tonality of a passage in which you hear several C sharps you might find it easier to think of a modulation to D major then translate this into a modulation to the dominant. Although the music you hear will be harmonised you should realise that tonal relationships can be established by the melody alone, so it would be sensible to take advantage of the clues that might be contained in the melodic lines printed in the skeleton score. Thus, if you know that the tonic key is F major, and you are asked to identify the key at a point where the melodic phrase cadences on a G, it would be silly to suggest that the music had modulated to D minor (since neither chord I nor chord V of D minor contains a G).

Harmony

You will also be tested on your ability to recognise a range of chords. Those that most clearly define tonality are:

- the tonic (I) and its first and second inversions (Ib and Ic),
- the subdominant (IV) and its first inversion (IVb),
- the dominant (V) and dominant 7th (V^7) and their first inversions (Vb and V^{7}b respectively).

To identify these chords you need to have mental images of them so that you can compare what you hear with what you have stored in your brain. The best way to create these aural images is to *sing* the chords as arpeggios using their letter names (including any sharps or flats) as your text.

The following example shows a way of turning chords I, IV and V^7 in root position into a melody that begins and ends on the tonic. If you or a friend can accompany the last three notes of the tune with chords Ic, V (or V^7) and I, you will become familiar with the most characteristic perfect cadence of the late-18th century. Sing this melody to the letter names of the chords in the key of G major.

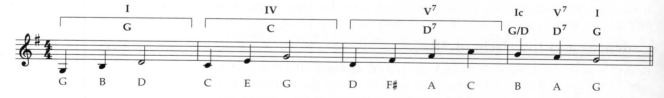

Once you have memorised the exercise you ought to be able to practise it almost anywhere without singing out loud (you will have internalised sound and symbol in the same way you internalise words when reading silently).

Now familiarise yourself with this progression in all the keys you might encounter in the AS exam. Do this by transposing it up in successive perfect fifths until you reach E major (if you are singing out loud you will need to drop an octave at some point or you will go into orbit!). The third note of the melody will always give you the tonic for each new key. Thus, when you transpose the exercise up a fifth to D major, you should sing D–F#–A (chord I), G–B–D (chord IV), A–C#–E–G (chord V^7), then F#–E–D.

Now transpose the melody down in successive perfect fifths until you reach the key of A♭ major. This time you can find the tonic of each new key by starting an octave below the fourth note of the melody. Thus, when you transpose the exercise down a fifth to C major you should sing C–E–G (chord I), F–A–C (chord IV), G–B–D–F (chord V^7), and then E–D–C.

Once you are confident, try the exercise in minor keys – use the harmonic rather than the melodic minor scale (e.g. G–Bb–D, C–Eb–G, D–F#–A–C, Bb–A–G in the key of G minor). Remember always to sing (out aloud or in your head) the exercise using the letter names of the key you have chosen to practise.

These are exercises you can do on your own, without an instrument and in any spare moments you have available. Once you have mastered them you should find it easy to identify the three primary triads and you will have experienced the effect of modulation to the dominant (rising fifths) and subdominant (falling fifths) many, many times over.

Inversions of chords I, IV, V and V^7

Get a friend to sing or play the following bass part to the exercise we have been working on, while you sing the melody:

I	Ib	IV	IVb	Vb	V	I	V^7	I

If you do this several times you will soon realise that first inversion chords (Ib, IVb, Vb or V^{7}b) are variants of the root position chords with which they are coupled (the only significant difference is that the third instead of the root is sounded in the bass). You need to be absolutely sure about this harmonic progression before you start to transpose it into other keys. For the bass part you should adopt the same method of transposition we have already described. So, in D major, for instance, the bass will be D (I), F# (Ib), G (IV), B (IVb), C# (Vb), A (V), D (I), A (V^7), D (I).

Secondary triads and the diminished 7th

Chords I, IV and V are called the primary triads. All other triads are known as secondary triads and the only ones you need to be able to identify for the AS Listening Paper are II and VI in root position.

In major keys chords II and VI are both minor triads so they are easy to distinguish from the major chords we discussed above. For instance, in the key of C major chord II is a triad of D minor (D–F–A) while chord VI is a triad of A minor (A–C–E).

Telling these two triads apart is a different matter, especially if you are asked to identify them as isolated chords rather than as a chord that forms an approach to a cadence. But remember what we said above about context. If the melody note is given you stand a good chance of being able to work out which of these secondary triads is being used since they only share one note in common.

In minor keys chord II is quite rare – it is a nasty sounding diminished triad, so should be obvious if it does occur in a test. In minor keys chord VI is a bright-sounding major triad the effect of which is quite unlike chord V (chords I and IV are, of course, minor triads in a minor key).

You should also be prepared to recognise the diminished 7th – a chord which usually contains at least one chromatic note, except when it occurs on the leading note of a minor key (e.g. Bb–D–F–Ab in C minor). It therefore has a distinctive colour which can sound a little exotic, as with the second chord of *NAM 23*, or that is sometimes associated with anguish as in bar 12 on page 296 of *NAM* (*Schmerz* means 'pain').

Cadences and the circle of 5ths

Both the **perfect cadence** (V–I) and the **plagal cadence** (IV–I) sound conclusive (like a phrase that ends with a full stop). You should have little trouble telling them apart if you can recognise these three chords.

The unexpected effect of an **interrupted cadence** can be experienced by ending the example above on a chord of E minor instead of G major, although it is important to remember that the second chord of the cadence does not have to be VI – it can be any chord other than a dominant chord.

The **imperfect cadence** ends with chord V. Since chord V needs eventually to resolve to chord I it marks the end of a phrase that makes only partial musical sense. In this cadence any chord other than those containing the leading note can come before chord V (in one past paper an exotic chromatic chord was used). You can, however, get a firm impression of the effect of an imperfect cadence by singing the first nine notes of the example opposite. You will immediately feel that chord V (the first three notes of bar 3) needs to be resolved by the perfect cadence implied by the last four notes of this melody.

Remember that perfect and imperfect cadences tend to occur much more frequently than interrupted and plagal cadences. In addition to cadences you should be prepared to recognise chord progressions based on the circle of fifths – a harmonic sequence consisting of chords whose roots are a 5th apart. In reality a circle of 5ths usually occurs as alternate rising 4ths and falling 5ths, as in *NAM 14*, bars 36–41.

This test is based on an extract from an oratorio by Handel.   *CD 1 track 4*
Take two minutes to study the single-stave skeleton score and the questions,
then listen to the first 43 seconds of the track FOUR TIMES as you answer the questions.

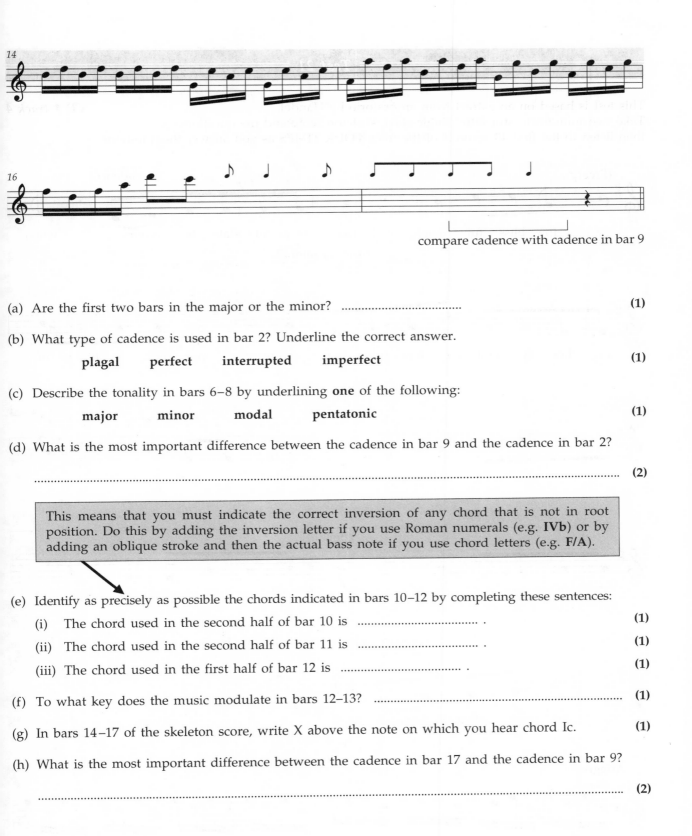

compare cadence with cadence in bar 9

(a) Are the first two bars in the major or the minor? .... **(1)**

(b) What type of cadence is used in bar 2? Underline the correct answer.

       plagal   **perfect**   **interrupted**   **imperfect**   **(1)**

(c) Describe the tonality in bars 6–8 by underlining **one** of the following:

       major   **minor**   **modal**   **pentatonic**   **(1)**

(d) What is the most important difference between the cadence in bar 9 and the cadence in bar 2?

.... **(2)**

> This means that you must indicate the correct inversion of any chord that is not in root position. Do this by adding the inversion letter if you use Roman numerals (e.g. **IVb**) or by adding an oblique stroke and then the actual bass note if you use chord letters (e.g. **F/A**).

(e) Identify as precisely as possible the chords indicated in bars 10–12 by completing these sentences:

    (i)   The chord used in the second half of bar 10 is ....   **(1)**

    (ii) The chord used in the second half of bar 11 is ....   **(1)**

    (iii) The chord used in the first half of bar 12 is ....   **(1)**

(f) To what key does the music modulate in bars 12–13? .... **(1)**

(g) In bars 14–17 of the skeleton score, write X above the note on which you hear chord Ic.   **(1)**

(h) What is the most important difference between the cadence in bar 17 and the cadence in bar 9?

.... **(2)**

Total: 12 marks

This test is based on the music for a hymn.
The excerpt is taken from timings 0:46 to 1:40 on CD 1 track 7.
The first 46 seconds contain an introductory fanfare which does not form part of this test.

CD 1 track 7

Take two minutes to study the single-stave skeleton score and the questions,
then listen to this excerpt FOUR TIMES as you answer the questions.

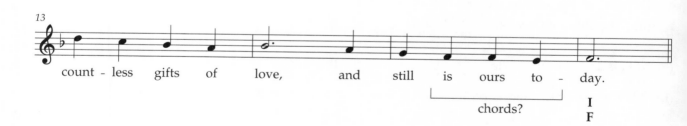

(a) The first two phrases each begin with chord I (F) and this has been marked on the score. Choose symbols from the following list to identify the chords indicated in bars 1 and 3.

Either	I	Ib	Ic	II	IV	IVb	V	Vb	VI
or	F	F/A	F/C	Gm	B♭	B♭/D	C	C/E	Dm

(i) The first chord in bar 1 is chord ....

(ii) The second chord in bar 1 is chord ....

(iii) The third chord in bar 1 is chord ....

(iv) The first chord in bar 3 is chord ....   **(4)**

(b) Name the cadences in:

(i) bars 5–6 ....

(ii) bar 8 ....   **(2)**

(c) What is the key of bars 9–10? Answer the question by underlining one of the following:

tonic   **tonic minor**   **relative minor**   **dominant**   **(1)**

(d) Tick **one** statement below which you think best describes the music for the phrase *hath blessed us on our way* (bars 10–12):

It ends with a perfect cadence in a major key.

It ends with a perfect cadence in a minor key.

It ends with an imperfect cadence in a major key.

It ends with an imperfect cadence in a minor key.   **(1)**

(e) Identify as precisely as possible the following chords in bar 15:

(i) The chord on beat 2. ....   **(1)**

(ii) The chord on beat 3. ....   **(1)**

(ii) The chord on beat 4. ....   **(2)**

Total: 12 marks

[39]

This test is based on an extract of chamber music by Beethoven.
Take two minutes to study the single-stave skeleton score and the questions,
then listen to the first 28 seconds of the track FOUR TIMES as you answer the questions.

Note that the first section of this extract (up to the double bar) is repeated.

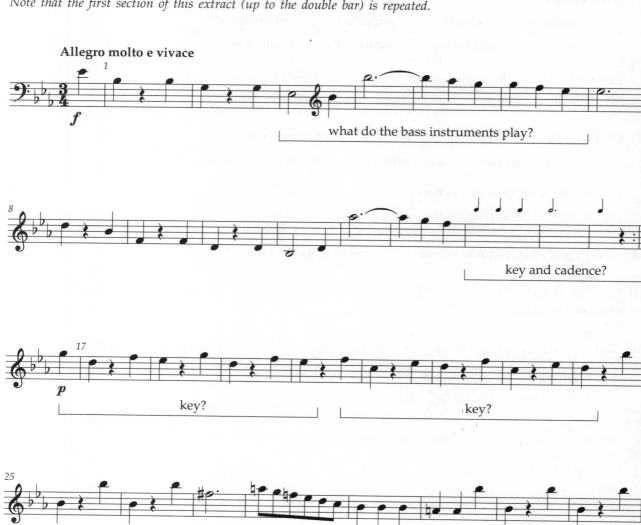

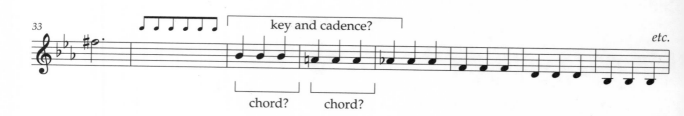

(a) Underline **two** terms below that most accurately describe the bass part in bars 3–6.

        tonic   dominant   major   minor

        scale   arpeggio   pedal   chord   **(2)**

(b) Using appropriate words from the following list identify the keys and cadences in the bars given below:

        perfect   **plagal**   **imperfect**   **interrupted**

        tonic   **tonic minor**   **dominant**   **relative minor**

    (i)   bars 15–16:   key .... cadence ....   **(2)**

    (ii)   bars 36–37:   key .... cadence ....   **(2)**

(c) Choosing from the following list, complete the sentences below:

        relative minor   **tonic minor**   **dominant**   **tonic**

    (i)   In bars 17–20 the key is the ....   **(1)**

    (ii)   In bars 21–24 the key is the .... ,   **(1)**

(d) Identify the chords in bars 35 and 36 as precisely as possible:

    (i)   bar 35 ....   **(1)**

    (ii)   bar 36 ....   **(1)**

(e) Complete the following sentence, which refers to the last three staves of the score only:

A passage in the bass using four consecutive pitches from an ascending chromatic scale

begins in bar .... and ends in bar ....   **(2)**

Total: 12 marks

This test is based on a song by C. V. Stanford.   *CD 2 track 19*
Take two minutes to study the single-stave skeleton score and the questions,
then listen to the first 80 seconds of the track FOUR TIMES as you answer the questions.

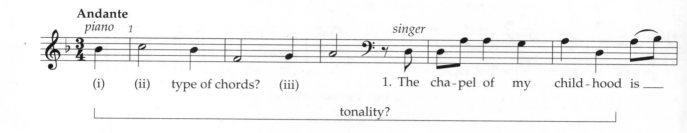

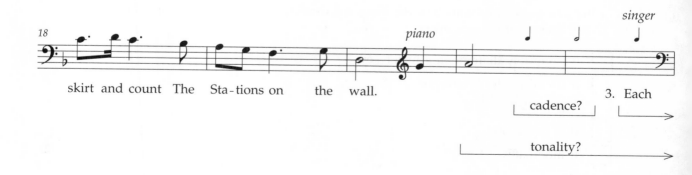

[42]

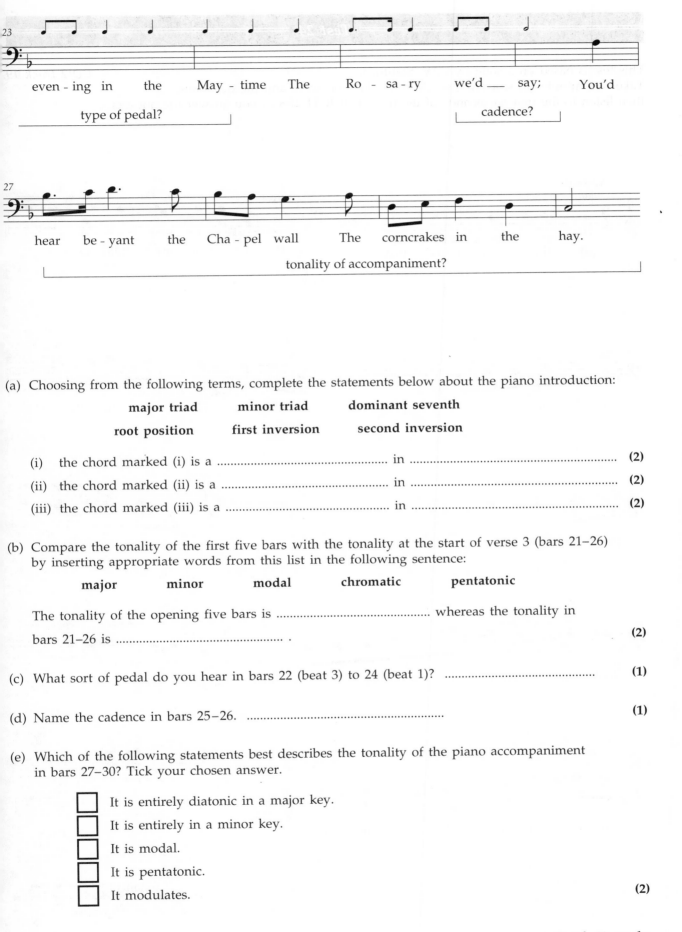

(a) Choosing from the following terms, complete the statements below about the piano introduction:

major triad **minor triad** **dominant seventh**

root position **first inversion** **second inversion**

    (i)   the chord marked (i) is a .... in .... **(2)**

    (ii) the chord marked (ii) is a .... in .... **(2)**

    (iii) the chord marked (iii) is a .... in .... **(2)**

(b) Compare the tonality of the first five bars with the tonality at the start of verse 3 (bars 21–26) by inserting appropriate words from this list in the following sentence:

    major   **minor**   **modal**   **chromatic**   **pentatonic**

The tonality of the opening five bars is .... whereas the tonality in

bars 21–26 is .... **(2)**

(c) What sort of pedal do you hear in bars 22 (beat 3) to 24 (beat 1)? .... **(1)**

(d) Name the cadence in bars 25–26. .... **(1)**

(e) Which of the following statements best describes the tonality of the piano accompaniment in bars 27–30? Tick your chosen answer.

    ☐   It is entirely diatonic in a major key.

    ☐   It is entirely in a minor key.

    ☐   It is modal.

    ☐   It is pentatonic.

    ☐   It modulates. **(2)**

Total: 12 marks

[43]

This test is based on an aria by Vivaldi.

The excerpt is taken from timings 1:11 to 2:33 on CD 2 track 6.

The first 70 seconds contain an introductory recitative which does not form part of this test.

CD 2 track 6

Take two minutes to study the single-stave skeleton score and the questions,
then listen to this excerpt FOUR TIMES as you answer the questions.

[44]

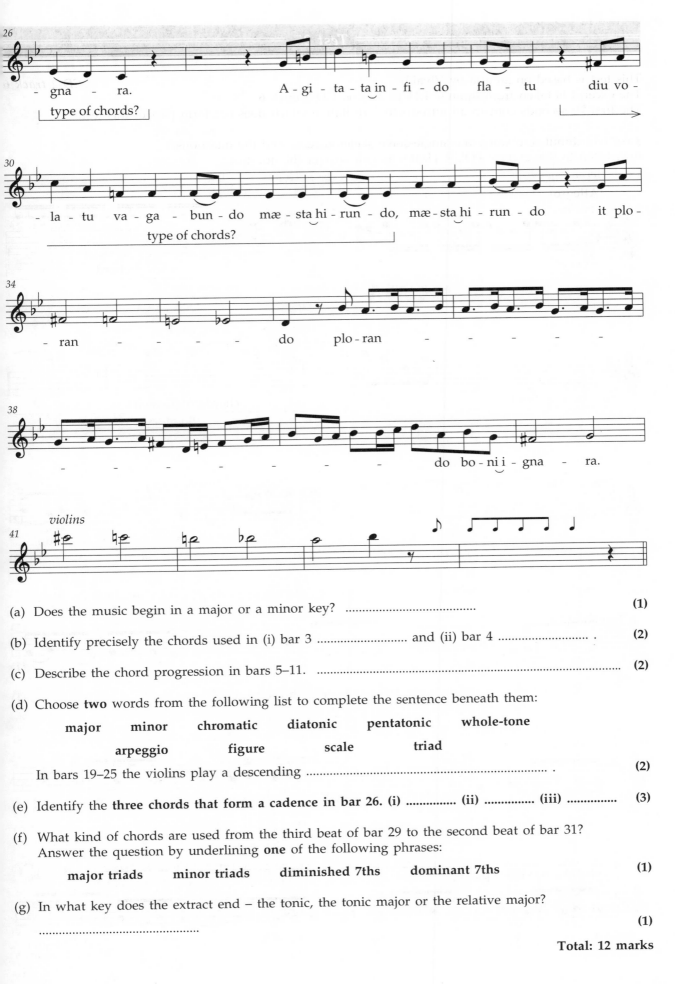

(a) Does the music begin in a major or a minor key? .... **(1)**

(b) Identify precisely the chords used in (i) bar 3 .... and (ii) bar 4 .... **(2)**

(c) Describe the chord progression in bars 5–11. .... **(2)**

(d) Choose **two** words from the following list to complete the sentence beneath them:

    major   minor   chromatic   diatonic   pentatonic   whole-tone

        arpeggio   figure   scale   triad

    In bars 19–25 the violins play a descending .... **(2)**

(e) Identify the **three chords that form a cadence in bar 26.** (i) .... (ii) .... (iii) .... **(3)**

(f) What kind of chords are used from the third beat of bar 29 to the second beat of bar 31?
    Answer the question by underlining **one** of the following phrases:

    major triads   minor triads   diminished 7ths   dominant 7ths **(1)**

(g) In what key does the extract end – the tonic, the tonic major or the relative major?

    .... **(1)**

                                                   Total: 12 marks

This test is based on a slow march by Purcell. It consists of five phrases and the entire piece is repeated.

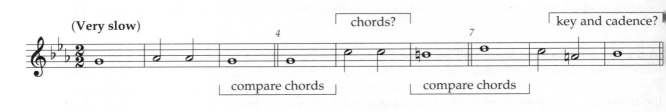

CD 1 track 19

Take two minutes to study the single-stave skeleton score and the questions, then listen to the track FOUR TIMES as you answer the questions.

The performers play the music a semitone higher than the pitch shown in this score.

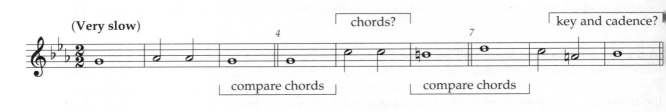

(a) Compare the chords in bars 3 and 4 by completing the missing words in this sentence:

The chord in bar 3 is .... whereas the chord in bar 4 is .... **(2)**

(b) Identify precisely the **two** chords in bar 5: first chord .... second chord .... **(2)**

(c) Compare the chords in bars 6 and 7 by completing the missing words in this sentence:

The chord in bar 6 is .... whereas the chord in bar 7 is .... **(2)**

(d) (i) Is phrase 3 (bars 7–9) in a major or a minor key? .... **(1)**

(ii) What kind of cadence occurs at the end of this phrase (in bars 8–9)? .... **(1)**

(e) Name the key of bars 10–12 and the cadence at the end of this phrase, using terms chosen from the following list.

        tonic   tonic major   relative major

    perfect   imperfect   plagal   interrupted

Key .... Cadence .... **(2)**

(f) Apart from length, state how the final chord of the entire piece (marked *y* in the score) differs from the last chord at the end of the first playing (marked *x*) by completing this sentence:

Chord *x* .... while chord *y* .... **(2)**

Total: 12 marks

5. Context

Chapters 5, 6 and 7 of this book refer to the three questions that occur in the A2 Music Listening Paper. For the examination you will be given an individual CD containing recordings of the extracts. You are allowed to play this as many times as you wish during the exam. It is important to pace yourself carefully, remembering that the final question carries more than half the marks. You should therefore allow ample time for this question, and you may want to consider tackling it first. Remember also to allow a few minutes to check your answers at the end, ensuring that you have not missed anything and that you have crossed-out any rough work that you do not want marked.

In the Context question there will be **three** different passages of music and no music notation for you to follow. You will be asked about the style and/or genre of each passage. The word 'genre' is pronounced *jon-rr* and refers to a category of things. One musical genre, for example, is the piano sonata, another is the madrigal. You may also be asked to suggest a date when the music was written and the name of its composer or (particularly in the case of jazz and pop music) the name of its performer.

Since identification may be required in several questions (including option B in AS Listening question 3) let's consider this issue in detail. There are many different styles of music, but the examiners are likely to limit themselves to representative examples from the following main areas of music:

Art music	Jazz and Pop
Renaissance (*c.*1450–1600) Baroque (*c.*1600–1750) Classical (*c.*1750–1825) Romantic (*c.*1825–1900) Modern styles of the 20th and 21st centuries, including: Impressionism (e.g. *NAM 5*) Expressionism (e.g. *NAM 40*) Neo-classicism (e.g. *NAM 7*) Serialism (e.g. *NAM 8*) Post-modernism (e.g. *NAM 32*) and Minimalism (e.g. *NAM 12*)	Ragtime and early jazz Swing and Big Band jazz Bebop jazz Modern jazz Blues Country and Western Gospel and Soul Pop Rock

The extracts on the CDs accompanying this book are mostly from the renaissance, baroque, classical and romantic periods but you will find examples of jazz and pop in our earlier book, *Aural Matters*.

Notice the little *c.* before the dates in the table above. It's an abbreviation of the Latin *circa* meaning 'approximately'. Changes in style did not happen in any one single year, so you will find some composers continuing to use a renaissance style for some years after 1600, just as you will find that some music written in the period just before 1600 anticipates features of the baroque style.

When mentioning dates, remember that in English the 16th century means 1500–1599, the 17th century means 1600–1699, and so on. One of the most common mistakes is to think that the year 1750, for example, is in the 17th century. It is not, it is in the 18th century.

To identify a piece of music it is essential to weigh-up *all* the evidence – the instruments and/or voices involved and how they are employed, the way that melody, rhythm and harmony have been used, the use of tonality, the presence of special features such as note-rows or blue notes, and so on. Never rely on just one or two features. For instance, much renaissance church music, such as *NAM 26*, has Latin words and is sung *a capella*. *NAM 30* also fits that description – and yet it is from the romantic period, as revealed by its dramatic contrasts, with wide leaps and chromatic movement in its melodic lines.

In the next few pages we have summarised various musical features that should help you to recognise some important styles and genres. We have had to be very selective and make many generalisations – so do not be surprised to find exceptions to what we write.

Recognising style and genre is something that becomes easier as you get to know more and more music, but it does require extensive listening. Make a habit of tuning into radio stations such as Classic FM, BBC Radio 3 and Jazz FM, and try to identify what you hear. You can do the same with the free CDs on the covers of music magazines and with sample tracks available on various web sites. No wild guessing, mind – rationalise your decisions by mentally listing the precise features that lead to your conclusions.

16th-century music

This century has often been called the golden age of renaissance music. Composers of the time include Palestrina and Lassus, both of whom worked on the continent, and a number of famous English composers, including Tallis, Byrd, Morley, Weelkes, Gibbons and Dowland.

Sacred music

The two most common genres of church music with Latin words are the **motet** and the Mass. These compositions were intended for small all-male choirs and are now usually sung *a capella*, as in the recording of *NAM 26* (page 266). After the Church of England broke from Rome in the mid-16th century, English became the normal language for services. The **anthem** has English words, but is musically similar to the Latin motet at this time. Important features of the style of late renaissance church music include:

- melodies that feature **stepwise** movement and that often form graceful arch-like contours (*NAM 26*, treble, bars 33–37). When there are leaps the melodic line usually returns within the leap to preserve the smoothly flowing movement that is so characteristic of renaissance sacred style.

- harmony based on root position and first-inversion triads (these are the only types of chord used in *NAM 26*). The most characteristic type of dissonance is the suspension in which a note in one part is held so that when another part moves a discord is formed. This discord is resolved when the first part moves by step to a concord (see right).

- **modality**, often modified at cadences to what sounds to our ears like major/minor tonality. For instance, in bar 60 of *NAM 26* there is a modal E♭ in the treble, but the phrase ends with E♮–F in bars 62–63, forming what appears to be a cadence in F major. In compositions in a minor key or mode, important sections nearly always end on a bare octave, a bare 5th or a major triad. The sharpened third in the last of these is known as a **tierce de Picardie** (*tierce* is French for third). Sometimes a Picardy third is immediately followed by a minor third in another part, forming a **false relation**. This striking effect can be heard between the top two parts in bars 28-29 (F♯ and F♮) of *NAM 26*.

- **imitative counterpoint** of the type heard in bars 56–57 of *NAM 26*. In some pieces successions of imitative entries disguise cadences and create a continuous web of contrapuntal sound – listen to *CD1 track 6* of the CDs that accompany this book. Although contrapuntal textures of this sort are typical of 16th-century sacred music, there are also numerous examples of homophony.

Secular music

The most famous type of secular (non-religious) vocal music of the renaissance is the **madrigal**. Established in Italy, the invention of music printing helped the genre to become known in other European countries, not least in England where madrigals are still associated with the age of Shakespeare and Queen Elizabeth I. Madrigals on more serious topics often share the features of sacred music outlined above but *NAM 34* (page 349) is a more jolly type of madrigal known as a ballett which, as its name suggests, imitated the style of instrumental dance music. Ballett style includes:

- fast triple metre with dancing dotted rhythms throughout.

- **syncopation** in, for instance, bars 9 (tenor) and 12 (alto). The complicated rhythm in the alto part of bars 21–22 is an example of a **hemiola** in which two printed bars in triple time effectively sound like three duple-time bars.

- systematic sharpening of certain notes. This leads to a much more **tonal style** than is common in most sacred music of the period: e.g. the use of F♯ makes *NAM 34* sound as though it is mainly in G major.

- contrapuntal textures. Those in *NAM 34* are based on the imitative treatment of short bouncy **motifs** rather than the long solemn melodies that are often found in sacred music.

- *fa-la-la* refrains and repeated sections.

The most popular type of solo song in England in 1600 was the **ayre** (notice the spelling), usually accompanied on the lute, as in the example by Dowland in *NAM 33* (page 347). Renaissance instrumental works included keyboard music for harpsichord (or virginals), such as the piece by Byrd on *CD1 track 16* of the CDs that accompany this book. Also popular was the type of chamber-music group known as a consort that can be heard in *NAM 13* (page 191). They are playing the most common type of Elizabethan dance music – a slow, duple-time pavane paired with a lively, triple-metre galliard.

Baroque music

If you compare *NAM 34* with *NAM 35* on page 353 (an Italian madrigal by Monteverdi) you will be amazed at the difference between these two pieces first published within four years of each other. Monteverdi was one of the earliest composers of **opera** and much of his music is imbued with the drama of this new art form. In *NAM 35* note lengths are governed by the natural rhythms of spoken Italian and melodic lines are designed for the dramatic expression of the text. Where discords in Renaissance music were carefully prepared and resolved, Monteverdi uses them blatantly for dramatic effect as in the first two entries of the uppermost parts. Extreme dissonance and chromaticism permeate the work.

Monteverdi was appointed choirmaster at St Mark's, Venice in 1613. His predecessor was Giovanni Gabrieli, composer of *NAM 27* (page 269). This work also shows many signs of the newly-emerging baroque style, including florid ornamentation and solo singers dramatically contrasted with various different choral and instrumental groupings. These are known as *cori spezzati* (divided choirs) and the type of music is known as polychoral (multiple choirs) – in both cases 'choirs' means groups of musicians, whether singers or instrumentalists. In the echoing spaces of St Mark's these resources were deployed around the various galleries to create a 'surround sound' effect. Most significant in *NAM 27* is the *basso per l'organo*. This is an early example of a **continuo** part – one of the most important innovations of the baroque era.

The late baroque

The period from 1675 to 1750 was the age first of Corelli and Purcell, and then of Vivaldi, Bach and Handel. By now the last vestiges of modality had given way to the major/minor system of tonality, which began to be used as a way to impose a clear sense of **form**. *NAM 15* (page 200) is a **trio sonata** which illustrates a number of features of the late baroque style:

- a **structure defined by key** – the first half of the binary form modulates from tonic to dominant, the second modulates back to the tonic, via other related keys, including a **cycle of 5ths** in bars 32–35.

- the pre-eminence of the **violin family** in all kinds of ensemble music.

- a **fugal texture** of two melody instruments playing high above a bass part, the intervening 'gap' being filled by the improvisation of one or more chordal continuo instruments (here an organ).

- a style based on the exploitation of just a few **melodic motifs** heard at the start.

- the unceasing **driving rhythm** of a lively gigue (one of several baroque dances discussed below).

Trio sonatas were one of the most common types of baroque chamber music. Another popular genre was the **suite** – a collection of movements mainly in different dance styles. Such works were written for solo instruments (especially the harpsichord) and for orchestra (Handel's *Fireworks Music* being a famous example). *NAM 21* (page249) consists of two dances from a suite by Bach – a slow, triple-time sarabande (much of it built upon a **walking bass** of continuous quavers) and a fast compound-time gigue. Notice how so many of the comments above on Corelli's gigue also apply to this example by Bach. The dances of the suite are usually in binary form, and feature many different speeds and rhythm patterns. The most popular dances were the allemande, courante, sarabande, minuet, gavotte, bourrée and gigue.

The baroque period also saw some of the earliest orchestral music, usually written for an ensemble of strings and continuo. Oboes and bassoons were often included, and trumpets and timpani sometimes feature in ceremonial music. One of the most common types of orchestral music was the **concerto**, which was based on the alternation of loud tutti sections and quieter passages that feature one or more soloists. By the time Vivaldi's famous set of concertos called *The Four Seasons* was published (*c*.1725) concertos were often written in three movements, in the order fast–slow–fast. Bach's fourth Brandenburg concerto features three soloists, and the first movement is printed as *NAM 1* (page 7). Numerous stylistic features identify this music as late baroque. Amongst the most important are:

- the spinning out of motifs to form extended melodies,

- the thorough exploitation of motifs from the opening ritornello even in the solo episodes,

- the density of the counterpoint (very evident in the complex **cross rhythms** at the end of every ritornello),

- sequential modulations (eg bars 35–43),

- idiomatic and **virtuoso** solo parts – for instance, the violin part in bars 83–137 fits the instrument like a glove but would be very difficult as the right hand part of a keyboard work,

- the sheer length and complexity of a movement which depends on a crystal clear tonal structure.

NAM 36 (page 356) illustrates two of the most important operatic genres of the baroque era. The first eight bars are a **recitative**, while the remainder is an air on a ground bass. An air simply means a formal song, and is known as an **aria** in Italian. A recitative and duet from an **oratorio** by Handel can be found on *CD1 track 4* of the CDs that accompany this book. Most of Handel's oratorios consist of settings in English of texts from the bible, the most famous being *Messiah* (1742). They were written for soloists, choir and orchestra and included many of the same genres as opera, but they were intended for concert performance, not for presentation on stage or for performance in church.

Another type of baroque vocal music that drew upon operatic genres was the **cantata**. *NAM 28* (page 288) contains four movements from a sacred cantata by Bach. These works have words in German and most include movements based on chorales (German hymns of the type seen on page 297 of *NAM*).

Viennese classical music

The four principal composers of the classical era (*c*.1750–1825) are Haydn, Mozart, Beethoven and Schubert. This was the period when the harpsichord was replaced by the **piano**, and when **clarinets** and **horns** became regular members of the orchestra. The presence of any of these instruments is often an indication that the music dates from after 1750. By the end of the 18th century, larger orchestras typically consisted of two each of flutes, oboes, clarinets, bassoons, horns and trumpets, plus a pair of timpani and a fairly large body of string players. Concertos remained popular, and both Mozart and Beethoven added many fine piano concertos to the genre, but the most important type of purely orchestral music was the **symphony**. Developed by Haydn (see *NAM 2*, page 31), the symphony eventually became a substantial and highly dramatic genre, typically in four movements consisting of:

- an allegro (often preceded by a slow introduction),
- a slow movement,
- a minuet (or fast *scherzo*) with contrasting trio, and
- a fast finale.

Just as clarinets and horns provided middle-range instruments for the orchestra, so the viola started to be used as an independent middle voice in chamber music. Thus, the trio-sonata texture of two violins and cello was expanded by the addition of a viola, producing the **string quartet** – and rendering redundant the need for a harpsichord to fill out the harmony. The string quartet (*NAM 16*, page 202) is one of the most characteristic sounds of the classical period, and it shares (along with related genres such as the piano trio and string quintet) the multi-movement format of the symphony listed above. Another important multi-movement genre is the keyboard **sonata** – *NAM 22* is the first movement of a sonata by Mozart.

One of the most characteristic features of the classical style is **periodic phrasing** – the use of phrases of regular length (2, 4 or 8 bars), often employed in balanced pairs known as antecedent and consequent – or more simply as question and answer. This can be heard clearly in the introduction to *NAM 37* (page 359), in which the first four bars end with an imperfect cadence and are answered by the next four bars which end with a perfect cadence. A similar pattern is used for the start of the verse – the first four bars end on the dominant chord and are answered by four bars which then modulate to the dominant key. Many features of the classical style are illustrated in *NAM 22* (page 253):

- periodic phrasing (the melody of the first 10 bars falls into five 2-bar phrases but, being a more subtle piece than *NAM 37*, they are disguised by linking semiquaver figures),

- a focus on elegant melody that is often **conjunct** (scale-based) or **triadic**, and frequently developed from short motifs by the use of sequences and repetition,

- mainly **diatonic** melody with frequent **appoggiaturas** (the first melody note in every one of the first five bars is an appoggiatura) and occasional decorative chromatic notes (e.g. E♮ in bars 4 and 6),

- **functional** harmony – meaning that the chords establish clearly-defined keys by means of cadential progressions which also help to define the structure of the music. For instance the chord progression of the first four bars is I–ii–V⁷–I, immediately defining B♭ major, the tonic key.

- light, clear, homophonic textures – most of this movement uses just a two-part texture in which the melody is predominant and counterpoint (by now considered to be rather old-fashioned) is almost entirely absent. Notice the use of broken-chord, repeated-chord and Alberti-bass figures.

Towards the end of the classical period Beethoven was pushing the boundaries of the elegant classical style in new directions – compare the first movement of his famous 5th symphony with his much smaller-scale movement on *CD1 track 9* of the accompanying Hyperion CD. Both are in a gruff C minor, focusing more on motifs than melody. Both look forward to a new age of drama rather than elegance.

The leading composer of classical opera was Mozart – an aria from his 'Marriage of Figaro' can be found in *Aural Matters*. Finally, **NAM 29** (page 299) reveals that even in church music, classical composers such as Haydn adopted a symphonic approach in which the orchestra carries most of the musical argument.

Romantic music

In the 19th century orchestras became larger still, with the addition of trombones, tuba and more horns, additional woodwind such as the piccolo, cor anglais and contrabassoon, a range of percussion (including the bass drum, triangle and cymbals), one or more harps, and larger numbers of string players.

The romantic period (*c*.1825–1900) was an age of extremes and this is well represented by music in *NAM*. For a new middle-class market of amateur music-making thousands of miniature songs and poetic piano pieces were published, such as those in **NAM 23** (page 258). At the same time, Wagner persuaded mad King Ludwig of Bavaria to subsidise his gargantuan operas and even to build an opera house designed especially for the production of them (**NAM 4** on page 65 is the prelude to a five-hour opera!). It was a time too when, in their desire to express the most intimate moods or violent passions, composers went their own ways and developed widely differing styles. Some composers tended to specialise mainly in one type of music – Chopin in piano music, for example, or Wagner and Verdi in opera.

Romantic character pieces

NAM 23 consists of three of Schumann's *Scenes from Childhood* (1838). They are **character pieces** designed to express particular moods as succinctly as possible and a popular genre of the romantic period. The first of them is composed in the pattern ‖:A:‖:BA:‖ – this is a miniature version of the rounded binary form Bach used in the sarabande of **NAM 21** (page 249). Listen to the phrase structure and you will soon become aware that the melody divides into balanced two and four-bar phrases. The first four bars end with an imperfect cadence and the next four with a perfect cadence – the 'question and answer' phrasing of the classical style, in fact. So what *is* romantic about the style of these pieces? The answer lies in:

- the folk-like simplicity of the melody of the first piece,

- the detailed performing directions, and especially the changes of speed in the first and third pieces,

- the often chromatic harmony (e.g. the first bar of the first piece and the first two bars of the third),

- the technical demands made of the pianist in the second piece.

For other examples of romantic piano music, listen to the Mazurka by Chopin in *Aural Matters* and to **CD1 track 23** on the accompanying Hyperion CDs. The latter is a piano **transcription** by Liszt of a song by Rossini and is an example of the **virtuoso** style that became highly popular in the 19th century. Written for performance to an admiring audience in a concert hall, it is at the opposite end of the spectrum to Schumann's character pieces to be enjoyed around the family piano.

Romantic Lieder

Lieder (German romantic songs) were also performed by amateurs in the home. Schumann composed many songs, but probably the greatest composer of the **Lied** (singular) was Schubert – we have already mentioned him as a classical composer, but many of his last works look forward to the romantic style.

Schubert's most popular songs are those in which the piano accompaniment represents an important idea in the text, or even adds a new image not explicitly stated by the poet. In *Die Forelle* ('The Trout'), for instance, a rippling semiquaver figure heard throughout the song represents the rippling stream. If you havn't got a recording of the song listen to the fourth movement of the 'Trout' Quintet in which Schubert used the melody as the **theme** for a set of **variations**, the last of which is almost a direct transcription of the song. Compare 'The Trout' with *Der Doppelgänger* ('The Ghostly Double', **NAM 38**, page 361) and you will get some idea of the terrific range of emotions Schubert was able to express through the Lied. Notice particularly the way terror is represented through:

- extreme dynamics (*fff* at climaxes, *ppp* at the end),

- extremely chromatic harmony (e.g. bar 41),

- low, dark piano textures,

- modulation to distant keys (e.g. D♯ minor in bars 47–50).

Der Doppelgänger comes from a **song cycle** (a collection of related songs) called *Schwanengesang* ('swan song') composed in 1828. Another song from the same cycle can be found in *Aural Matters*, page 132.

Romantic opera

The romantic period was a great age for Italian opera, beginning with the works of Rossini and ending with the works of Verdi and Puccini (whose later operas date from the early 20th century). Although style changed considerably during this period, opera in the Italian language is characterised by writing designed at least in part as a display vehicle for the professional singer. A short excerpt from Verdi's *Otello* is included in *Aural Matters*. Wagner's operas, written in German, represent a very different tradition in which the orchestra plays a fundamental role in developing the drama in symphonic terms. *NAM 4* is the prelude to Wagner's *Tristan und Isolde*. A further excerpt from this opera can be found in *Sound Matters*.

Conservative romantics

Early romantic composers such as Mendelssohn and Schumann wrote symphonies, concertos and chamber music that reveal just how much of the romantic style grew from classical roots. In the second half of the 19th century Brahms continued this tradition. *NAM 18* (page 231) is the third movement of his Piano Quintet in F minor, and is a **scherzo and trio** – a form that can be found in many instrumental works by Haydn and Beethoven. The scherzo is in C minor – its stormy mood contrasts strongly with the lyrical style of the trio (which is in the **tonic major**). But if the genre and form are classical the style is definitely romantic and can be briefly illustrated by bars 176–190 in which the strings play the same motif together so it can be heard against the massive, syncopated piano chords, and aggressive discords are formed between the string parts and the Db-major chords of the piano part.

Revolutionary romantics

Composers such as Mendelssohn had written works that suggest pictorial images, such as his *Italian* and *Scottish* symphonies, but these images were only incidental to the traditional symphonic forms he used. Berlioz was much more revolutionary in his *Symphonie fantastique* of 1830. The very structure of this work was determined by the detailed story that it set out to portray in music. This story was a highly personal 'episode in the life of an artist' (i.e. Berlioz himself) which the composer had printed in concert programmes to help audiences understand the music. It gave rise to the expression **programme music** for pieces whose form is partly determined by a story or image that the composer intends to convey in sound. Later composers such as Liszt and Richard Strauss were to develop orchestral programme music into a new genre, known as the symphonic poem or **tone poem**.

Berlioz was a master of orchestration. All of the textures heard in the third movement of *Harold in Italy* (*NAM 3*, page 42) are crystal clear and the **timbres** of all the instruments shine through. Notice how he uses new instruments such as the cor anglais for the solo on page 44, and special effects such as the harp harmonics from page 61 onwards. Notice, too, how he achieves unusual orchestral colours by doubling solo instruments at the octave (e.g. piccolo and oboe at the start, or oboe, cor anglais and bassoon playing the same melody at three different pitch levels in bars 53–58).

The sub-title of *Harold in Italy* is 'Symphony in four movements with viola solo' and Berlioz gave each of the movements programmatic descriptions. Thus *Harold* combines elements of the symphony, concerto and tone poem. Such blurring of the boundaries of genres is a typical feature of much romantic music.

The modern era

The late romantic period includes many famous composers besides those we have already mentioned – such as Grieg, Tchaikovsky, Dvořák, Bizet and Saint-Saëns – and the romantic style continued into the early 20th century in the work of composers such as Elgar and Rachmaninov. But already in the years just before 1900 new styles were starting to appear in music as they were in the other arts. In this final section we will take a look at just a few of the many styles of the 20th and 21st centuries.

Impressionism

Just as impressionist painters used colour to suggest the play of light rather than to define shapes, so impressionist composers used sound to suggest visual or poetic images rather than to define form. To achieve this they radically modified most of the musical elements we have discussed earlier. An extreme example is Debussy's piano prelude called *Voiles* (quoted in *Sound Matters*, 37) which, being based on a **whole tone scale**, is almost entirely **atonal**. Only an insistently repeated Bb in the bass suggests a tonal centre, and even this is negated by the major third on middle C with which the prelude ends. This music dates from 1910, but impressionism can be dated back to 1894 when Debussy's exotic *Prélude à l'après-midi d'un faune* (*NAM 5*, page 86) was first performed. The most obvious ways in which traditional elements are radically modified in this piece include:

- avoidance of a perceptible beat (listen to the opening flute melody and try to conduct it!),
- chromatic and pentatonic melodies (bars 1–2 and 3–4 respectively),
- chords used for colour alone – e.g. the chord in bar 4 is E^6 (an E major triad with added 6th) and is totally unrelated to the Bb^7 in the next bar,
- consecutive parallel discords such as the seventh chords in the string parts in bar 37,
- new orchestral colours – e.g. muted violins *beneath* muted horns in bars 107–108, with low flutes and antique cymbals.

Expressionism and serialism

Instead of giving an *impression* of external images, expressionists sought to give *expression* to the inner-most workings of the human mind. In *Der kranke Mond* (*NAM 40*, page 364) nightmare images are evoked by:
- the deliberate avoidance of metre and tonality,
- the free use of dissonance (listen to the setting of the word *dort* in bar 3),
- angular melodic contours (listen to the flute part in bar 1),
- the use of a vocal technique (called *sprechstimme*) in which the text is half-said, half-sung and sometimes combined with deliberately exaggerated tremolo (last two bars).

The atonal style of works like *Pierrot Lunaire* (from which *NAM 40* is taken) led to **serialism** in which all pitches are treated equally and rule-based techniques replace the structural function of tonality. Such music is exceedingly difficult to analyse by ear, but you might be asked to comment on the textures such as that heard at the start of *NAM 8* (page 160) in which a series of detached timbres is spread over a wide pitch range. **Pointillist** textures like these were particularly exploited by Webern and later **modernist** composers such as Boulez and Stockhausen.

Neo-classicism

Neo-classicism refers to 20th-century music that was inspired by earlier musical styles. The excerpts from Stravinsky's ballet *Pulcinella* in *NAM 7* (page 139) are re-workings of 18th-century pieces but Shostakovich's Prelude and Fugue in A (*NAM 25*, page 262) is an original composition that is clearly inspired by Bach's 48 Preludes and Fugues. The Bachian contribution to the style of these pieces is seen in the use of a limited number of motifs throughout the prelude and the use of strict fugal techniques. But new creative elements are evident in the free treatment of dissonance in the prelude, the free treatment of modulation and tonality in both prelude and fugue, and (paradoxically) the complete avoidance of dissonance in the fugue.

Minimalism and post-modernism

In the second half of the 20th-century **minimalism** arose as a reaction against the complexity of modernist styles such as serialism. In his *New York Counterpoint* of 1985 (*NAM 12*, page 176), Steve Reich creates mesmerising textures with minimal melodic and harmonic resources (listen to the way the motifs heard at the start are shifted to different beats of the bar to create alternating major triads a step apart). A return to a type of tonality is evident in his use of all seven pitches of a major scale, but his use of nothing but clarinet timbre is clearly a rejection of the sumptuous orchestral textures of Wagner and Debussy – and his use of pre-recorded tape, while only obvious in a live performance, identifies this as modern music.

In fact minimalism turned out to be just one strand in the **post-modernist** return to tonality. Reich's latest works have signalled a renewal of traditional melodic styles and these are also evident in the more eclectic compositions of John Tavener. In his setting of Blake's 'Song of Innocence', *The Lamb* (*NAM 32*, page 344, also written in 1985) Tavener's eclecticism is apparent in using:
- an initial soprano melody of just four different pitches as the basis of the entire work,
- melodic inversion to create bitonality in bar 2 (where the alto is a mirror image of the soprano),
- 'cut and paste' techniques to form the melody of bar 3 from the soprano and alto pitches of bar 2,
- retrograde technique (bar 4 is a backwards version of bar 3),
- exchange of parts in bar 5 (compare soprano pitches 2–4 with alto pitches 5–7 and *vice versa*),
- modal homophony (all pitches of the aeolian mode on E are used in bars 7–10),
- an ametrical style based on word rhythms rather than a regular pulse,
- rhythmic augmentation (compare bar 10 with bar 9),
- traditional expressive techniques such as the double suspension on 'Lamb' in bars 9, 19 and 20.

This brief overview of 20th-century music has of necessity been very selective and omits such famous composers as Stravinsky and Britten whose music encompasses a range of styles. Jazz and popular music is not included in this book, so we recommend that you make sure you can recognise the styles of the various examples in *Aural Matters* (pages 73–97) and in the *New Anthology* (pages 461–518).

You can listen to the three recordings as many times as you wish, but we suggest that you aim to complete the test in no more than 10 minutes, making sure that you answer all nine questions in that time.

Excerpt A
Listen to the first 58 seconds of CD2 track 14

(a) Which of the following best describes this music? Underline your answer.

symphony   **sonata**   **waltz**   **nocturne**   **study**   **(1)**

(b) Give a reason to justify your answer to question (a).

.... **(1)**

(c) In which of the following years was this music composed? Underline **one** answer.

1599   **1699**   **1799**   **1899**   **1999**   **(2)**

Excerpt B
Listen to the first 56 seconds of CD2 track 16

(d) Which of the following best describes the style of this music? Underline one answer.

classical   **baroque**   **renaissance**   **neo-classical**   **minimalist**   **(1)**

(e) Give a reason to justify your answer to question (d).

.... **(1)**

(f) Name a likely composer of this music. .... **(2)**

Excerpt C
Listen to the first 55 seconds of CD2 track 15

(g) Place a tick against **one** statement about this music below that you believe is true.

☐ It is from a motet written for performance by a church choir in a religious service
☐ It is from a song written for performance on stage in an American musical
☐ It is from a quartet written for performance in a salon by four professional singers
☐ It is from a cantata written for performance in a concert hall by an amateur choir   **(1)**

(h) In which century was this music written? .... **(1)**

> Remember the advice about centuries that we gave on page 47.

(i) Give **two** reasons to justify your answer to question (h).

1. ....

2. .... **(2)**

Total: 12 marks

You can listen to the three recordings as many times as you wish, but we suggest that you aim to complete the test in no more than 10 minutes, making sure that you answer all nine questions in that time.

Excerpt A
Listen to the first 31 seconds of *CD2 track 22*

(a) Which of the following best describes this music? Underline your answer.

     anthem   ayre   cantata   lied   madrigal   motet   **(1)**

(b) Give the name of **one** composer who you think wrote the music. .... **(2)**

(c) Suggest a possible year of composition. .... **(1)**

Excerpt B
Listen to the first 60 seconds of *CD2 track 18*

(d) What type of choir is singing this excerpt? .... **(1)**

(e) Which of the following best describes this music? Underline your answer.

     anthem   ayre   cantata   lied   madrigal   motet   **(1)**

(f) Which of the following composers wrote this music? Underline your answer.

     Britten   **Byrd**   **Handel**   **Purcell**   **Elgar**   **Sullivan**   **(2)**

Excerpt C
Listen to the first 70 seconds of *CD2 track 7*

(g) On what style of traditional music is this arrangement based? .... **(1)**

(h) Place a tick against **one** statement below that you believe is true.

- [ ] The excerpt is from a 17th-century orchestral work
- [ ] The excerpt is from an 18th-century orchestral work
- [ ] The excerpt is from a 19th-century orchestral work
- [ ] The excerpt is from a 20th-century orchestral work **(1)**

(i) Justify your answer to question (h) by giving **two** reasons for your choice.

1. ....

2. .... **(2)**

Total: 12 marks

You can listen to the three recordings as many times as you wish, but we suggest that you aim to complete the test in no more than 10 minutes, making sure that you answer all nine questions in that time.

Excerpt A

Listen to the *last* 50 seconds of *CD2 track 12*
(from approximately 6:00 to the end of the track)

(a) Which of the following best describes this music? Underline your answer.

symphony concerto quartet tone poem overture   **(1)**

(b) Of which of the following periods is this music characteristic? Underline your answer.

renaissance   baroque   classical   romantic   **(1)**

(c) Why might this music be described as *virtuosic* in style?

.... **(2)**

Excerpt B

Listen to the first 55 seconds of *CD1 track 25*

(d) Which of the following best describes this music? Underline your answer.

anthem ayre cantata lied madrigal motet   **(1)**

(e) Name a likely composer of this music. .... **(2)**

(f) For what purpose was the piece composed?

.... **(1)**

Excerpt C

Listen to the first 41 seconds of *CD1 track 24*

(g) What type of dance music is this? .... **(1)**

(h) Place a tick against the decade in which you think this music was written.

□ 1590–1600
□ 1690–1700
□ 1790–1800
□ 1890–1900
□ 1990–2000   **(1)**

(i) Justify your answer to question (h) by giving **two** reasons for your choice.

1. ....

2. .... **(2)**

Total: 12 marks

You can listen to the three recordings as many times as you wish, but we suggest that you aim to complete the test in no more than 10 minutes, making sure that you answer all nine questions in that time.

Excerpt A
Listen to the first 50 seconds of *CD1 track 28*

(a) Which of the following best describes the style of this music? Underline your answer and then give one reason for your choice.

post-modernism   **serialism**   **impressionism**   **expressionism**   **neo-classicism**   **(1)**

reason: .... **(1)**

(b) Which of the following best describes the genre of this piece? Underline your answer.

madrigal   **lied**   **sacred music**   **chamber music**   **operetta**   **(1)**

(c) Underline the year in which you believe this music was written.

1909   **1929**   **1949**   **1969**   **(1)**

Excerpt B
Listen to the first 30 seconds of *CD1 track 22*

(d) This extract is taken from a sonatina (a little sonata) for flute and piano.
From which of the three movements of the sonatina is the extract is taken? .... **(1)**

(e) What type of music influenced the style of this flute sonatina? .... **(1)**

(f) Suggest the year in which this piece was written. .... **(2)**

Excerpt C
Listen to all of *CD1 track 11*

(g) The title of this piece means 'Far from home'. Which of the following best describes the genre of the music? Underline your answer.

march   **waltz**   **nocturne**   **minuet**   **study**   **character piece**   **(1)**

(h) For what purpose do you think this piece was written?

.... **(1)**

(i) Which of the following best describes the style of this music? Underline one answer.

romantic   **classical**   **baroque**   **renaissance**   **neo-classical**   **serial**   **(1)**

(j) Give **one** musical reason to justify your answer to question (i).

.... **(1)**

Total: 12 marks

6. Comparison

For the second question in the A2 Listening Paper there will be two passages of music which will be identified as Excerpt A and Excerpt B. There will not be any music notation for you to follow. You will have to answer questions about the similarities and differences between the two passages.

The two excerpts might come from different parts of the same piece – for instance, you might be asked to compare two different variations of the same theme, or to compare an opening section with the way it is changed when it returns later in the work. However, the comparison could be between two different pieces by the same composer (or band), or between two works by different composers that are in the same genre (e.g. two slow movements for string quartet, one by Mozart and one by Beethoven). It is also possible that you might be asked to comment on the similarities and differences between an original version of a piece and an arrangement (with significant changes) of the same work.

This activity is like the second question in the AS Listening Paper, but while that was solely concerned with the differences between two performances of the same music, this A2 question is about differences *in the music itself*. In addition, you should expect questions on *similarities* between the excerpts, although it is likely that there will be more differences to identify than similarities. Also, you may be asked to identify the music and perhaps to make deductions about how the extracts relate to each other, e.g. one might be a baroque original while the other is a 19th-century arrangement for larger resources.

Some questions may require you to write a short commentary. This can consist of just notes or bullet points, but it is essential that the points you make are very specific. For example, just claiming that one extract is 'more exciting' than the other is unlikely to impress the examiners. In order to get some marks you would need to cite specific evidence – for instance, you might state that extract B is more exciting because it starts with a crescendo for brass over a dominant pedal, whereas extract A begins with a quiet passage for strings over a tonic pedal. See page 65, question (e), for more help on this type of answer.

For some of the tests in this chapter you will need access to additional CDs. Once again, we have tried to make suggestions of recordings that should be reasonably easy to obtain.

Test 31

This test is based on a comparison of the first half of *CD1 track 16* (which we will call 'Excerpt A' and which lasts 36 seconds) with the remainder of the same track, which we will call Excerpt B. You can listen to the music as many times as you wish, but try to complete the test in no more than 15 minutes.

(a) Underline the word **TRUE** or **FALSE** in response to each of the following statements.

    (i)   Excerpt A is in compound time while Excerpt B is in simple time.   **TRUE   FALSE**   **(1)**

    (ii)   Excerpt A modulates from tonic to dominant.   **TRUE   FALSE**   **(1)**

    (iii) Excerpt B starts in the dominant and ends in the tonic.   **TRUE   FALSE**   **(1)**

    (iv) Both excerpts consist of phrases repeated in sequence.   **TRUE   FALSE**   **(1)**

    (v)   Both excerpts consist of phrases that are repeated with decorations.   **TRUE   FALSE**   **(1)**

    (vi) Both excerpts change tempo half way through.   **TRUE   FALSE**   **(1)**

(b) How are the excerpts related (i) melodically and (ii) harmonically?

    (i)   ....   **(1)**

    (ii) ....   **(1)**

(c) Underline the most likely composer of this music.

     Britten   **Brahms**   **Berlioz**   **Beethoven**   **Bach**   **Byrd**   **(2)**

(d) Identify **three** ways in which Excerpt B differs from Excerpt A.

1. ....

2. ....

3. .... **(6)**

Total: 16 marks

=== *Test 32* ===

This test is based on a comparison of *CD2 track 13*, which we will call 'Excerpt A', with *NAM 39*, which we will call Excerpt B. Do not follow the score in the *New Anthology* as you listen to the recording. You can listen to the music as many times as you wish, but try to complete the test in no more than 15 minutes.

(a) (i)   Suggest the year in which Excerpt A was written.   ....   **(1)**

(ii) Which one of the following is correct? Tick your choice.

☐   Excerpt B was composed at about the same time as Excerpt A.

☐   Excerpt B was composed about 60 years after Excerpt A.

☐   Excerpt B was composed about 60 years before Excerpt A.   **(2)**

(b) Both excerpts are French songs with piano accompaniment (a genre known as the *mélodie*). State **three** other ways in which they are similar.

1. ....

2. ....

3. .... **(3)**

(c) Indicate the excerpt that includes each of the following features by answering A or B.

(i)   An opening bass part that ascends chromatically.   ....   **(1)**

(ii) An opening that moves directly from the tonic chord to a diminished 7th.   ....   **(1)**

(iii) An opening based on a circle of 5ths.   ....   **(1)**

(iv) A vocal part that includes cross-rhythms with the accompaniment.   ....   **(1)**

(v) A vocal part that includes the frequent use of triplet rhythms.   ....   **(1)**

(vi) A vocal part that includes the frequent use of dotted rhythms.   ....   **(1)**

(d) Describe **two** ways in which the excerpts differ.
Do *not* repeat any of the points made in answer to question (c) above.

1. ....

....

2. ....

.... **(4)**

Total: 16 marks

This test is based on a comparison of **CD1 track 19**, which we will call 'Excerpt A', with **CD2 track 18**, which we will call Excerpt B.

You can listen to the music as many times as you wish, but try to complete the test in no more than 15 minutes.

(a) In which of the following periods were both excerpts written? Underline your answer.

    1575–1600   **1675–1700**   **1775–1800**   **1875–1900**   **1975–2000**   **(2)**

(b) Which one of the following is correct? Tick your choice.

    ☐ Excerpt A is in a key a semitone higher than Excerpt B.

    ☐ Excerpt A is in the same key as Excerpt B.

    ☐ Excerpt A is in a key a semitone lower than Excerpt B.   **(2)**

(c) State **two** ways in which the extracts are different in texture.

    1. ....

    2. .... **(4)**

(d) Complete the two sentences below using terms and phrases from the following list.

    perfect   **plagal**   **minor**   **major**   **an open 5th**   **a tierce de picardie**

Excerpt A ends with a .... cadence and the final chord of the piece is

.... Excerpt B ends with a .... cadence and

the final chord of the piece is .... **(4)**

(e) Identify **four** differences between the extracts not already mentioned above.

    1. ....

    2. ....

    3. ....

    4. .... **(4)**

Total: 16 marks

This test is based on a comparison of the first 1 minute and 46 seconds of a recording of the duet *La Regata Veneziana* from Rossini's *Soirées Musicales* (which we will call Excerpt A) with the first 82 seconds of **CD1 track 23** (which we will call Excerpt B).

For the former we used the version recorded by Victoria de los Angeles, Elisabeth Schwarzkopf and Gerald Moore on the bargain-priced CD 'Three Living Legends' (EMI Eminence CD EMX2233). This also includes a performance of Mendelssohn's duet *Ich wollt' meine Lieb'* that you could use for comparison with the performance of the same duet on **CD2 track 9** of the accompanying CDs.

You can listen to the music as many times as you wish, but try to complete the test in no more than 15 minutes.

(a) Excerpt A was written by Rossini. Which of the following composers arranged the music heard in Excerpt B? Underline your answer.

    Handel   **Mozart**   **Liszt**   **Wagner**   **Verdi**   **Stravinsky**   **Schoenberg**   **(1)**

(b) For Excerpt A, suggest a year of composition. .... **(1)**

(c) Which extract is performed at the slower tempo, A or B? .... **(1)**

(d) Underline the word **TRUE** or **FALSE** in response to each of the following statements.

  (i) Both excerpts start with an arpeggiated diminished 7th chord. **TRUE FALSE** **(1)**

  (ii) This opening arpeggio ends with a triplet rhythm in Excerpt B only. **TRUE FALSE** **(1)**

  (iii) Excerpt B is a semitone higher than Excerpt A. **TRUE FALSE** **(1)**

  (iv) Excerpt B has one less section than Excerpt A. **TRUE FALSE** **(1)**

  (v) Excerpt B is arranged for piano duet. **TRUE FALSE** **(1)**

(e) Briefly explain how the music of Excerpt A is incorporated into Excerpt B, considering the vocal parts, bass and chords.

  (i) vocal parts: .... **(1)**

  (ii) bass and chords: .... **(1)**

(f) Outline **three** other differences between the two versions, apart from any already mentioned above.

....

....

....

....

.... **(6)**

                       Total: 16 marks

This test is based on a comparison of the first 60 seconds of **CD2 track 8**, which we will call Excerpt A, with the first 37 seconds of **track 29** from the CD *Goldberg Variations* transcribed by Dmitry Sitkovetsky (Nonesuch/Warner, 7559-79341-2), which we will call Excerpt B.

For Excerpt B you could instead use the first 50 seconds of **track 29** from the Telarc CD that we used for Test 14, although obviously the similarities and differences will not all be the same with a different recording. Whichever CD you use will give you ample practice for this exam question, since any of the tracks can be compared with **CD8 track 8** on Hyperion CDs that accompany this book.

Listen to the music as many times as you wish, but try to complete the test in no more than 15 minutes.

(a) Complete the sentence below with terms chosen from the following list:

dominant   **tonic**   **subdominant**   **relative minor**   **relative major**   **tonic minor**

Both excerpts start on the .... chord of the tonic key and they both end in the

.... key.   **(2)**

(b) Underline the word **TRUE** or **FALSE** in response to each of the following statements.

   (i)   Both excerpts are in triple metre.   **TRUE   FALSE**   **(1)**

   (ii) Both excerpts begin with a phrase that is repeated an octave lower.   **TRUE   FALSE**   **(1)**

   (iii) Only excerpt B begins with a varied sequence.   **TRUE   FALSE**   **(1)**

   (iv) The melody in both excerpts consists of mainly stepwise movement.   **TRUE   FALSE**   **(1)**

   (v) Excerpt B is arranged for a string quartet.   **TRUE   FALSE**   **(1)**

   (vi) Both excerpts use essentially the same chord progression.   **TRUE   FALSE**   **(1)**

(c) (i) Excerpt B starts with an inner part not heard in Excerpt A. On which **two** of the following is that inner part based. Underline your answers.

           acciaccaturas   **trills**   **mordents**   **turns**

       dominant pedal   **tonic pedal**   **sequence**   **imitation**   **(2)**

   (ii) When this inner part stops for a few bars, how does the rhythm of the music compare with the parallel passage in Excerpt A?

      ....   **(1)**

   (iii) When the inner part resumes in the final bars of Excerpt B, state **two** ways in which it is different from its first appearance.

      1. ....   2. ....   **(2)**

(d) Listen carefully to the opening bars of each extract and then describe **three** ways (other than instrumentation) in which the bass part of Excerpt B differs from the bass part of Excerpt A.

....

....

....   **(3)**

                                       Total: 16 marks

This test is based on a comparison of the first 1 minute and 35 seconds of *CD2 track 12*, which we will call Excerpt A, with the opening 1 minute and 35 seconds of Liszt's Piano Concerto No.1 in Eb major, which we will call Excerpt B. For the latter we used a mid-price CD by Sviatoslav Richter and the London Symphony Orchestra (Philips Classics 464 710-2) but there are many other recordings of this work, and it is a piece that most music libraries are likely to have available.

Listen to the music as many times as you wish, but try to complete the test in no more than 15 minutes.

(a) This question refers to the opening bars of each extract (the first 12 seconds of Extract A and the first 15 seconds of Extract B) in which a scale-based motif is heard twice.

(i) In the table below write **A** or **B** or **BOTH** to show which feature is heard in which extract.

Played by strings (wind enter at ends of phrases)	
Dotted rhythms	
Trills	
Pauses	
A texture *entirely* of bare octaves	
A motif based on a descending chromatic scale	

(6)

(ii) The opening motif of Extract A is repeated in sequence in this opening passage. How precisely is it different from the first time it is heard?

.... **(2)**

(iii) The opening motif of Extract B is repeated in sequence in this opening passage. How precisely is it different from the first time it is heard?

.... **(2)**

(b) Name **two** differences between the extracts in the music immediately following this opening.

....

.... **(2)**

(c) Compare the way in which the opening motif is used in the remainder of the two extracts.

....

....

.... **(3)**

(d) Why do you think that Extract B has a more dramatic impact than Extract A?

.... **(1)**

Total: 16 marks

7. General Test of Aural Perception

In the final A2 question you will have one excerpt of music for which a two-stave skeleton score will be provided. There will be three questions on pitch and rhythm, of which you must answer **two**:
(a) three fragments of music will be printed, and you must locate where in the score each occurs,
(b) you will be asked to notate the rhythm of a short passage heard on the CD,
(c) you will be asked to notate the pitches of a short melody heard on the CD (the rhythm will be given).

You must also answer **two** other questions:
(d) you will have to identify keys, key relationships, chords or chord progressions in the extract,
(e) you will have to write a short commentary on the music and place the extract in context.

Recordings and skeleton scores

Before attempting the tests in this chapter carefully check the score, paying particular attention to:
- clefs (do they change anywhere?)
- key signatures (do they relate to a major or a minor key?)
- time signatures (simple or compound time?)
- tempo marks.

The tempo mark and time signature should give you a clue to the type of note that represents the beat. For instance, in slow $\frac{6}{8}$ time the beat is usually a quaver (six beats per bar, as in *NAM 4*), but at a fast tempo the beat is likely to be a dotted crotchet (two beats per bar, as in *NAM 15*). Be aware that a slow beat may be represented by short time values (such as in the last movement of *NAM 28*, where the beat is a quaver), and that a fast beat may be represented by long note values (e.g. *NAM 13*, page 193).

It's important to understand these ideas because the beat will help you keep your place in the score while you concentrate on listening for the features required in the questions. It is particularly difficult to do this when melodic contours are replaced by rhythmic patterns extending over several bars. The best way to understand the relationships between metre, tempo and notation is to conduct music you hear while following the score. Try this out with the following passages from the *New Anthology*:
- Simple duple metre: *NAM 25* Fugue, pages 263–5, ¢ ($\frac{2}{2}$), slow minim beat
- Simple triple metre: *NAM 28* Aria, pages 297–9, $\frac{3}{8}$, moderate quaver beat
- Simple quadruple metre: *NAM 27* pages 269–70, $\frac{4}{2}$, slow minim beat
- Compound duple metre: *NAM 7* Variation 1, pages 151–2, $\frac{6}{8}$, moderate dotted-crotchet beat
- Compound triple metre: *NAM 21* Gigue, pages 251–2, $\frac{9}{16}$, very fast dotted-quaver beat
- Compound quadruple metre: *NAM 25* Prelude, pages 262–3, $\frac{12}{8}$, moderate dotted-crotchet beat

Question (a)

In order to spot the fragments (which could be in treble, alto or bass clefs, or which could be rhythmic) it is vital that you have a mental image of their *sound*. The most musical way to achieve this is to try singing, however approximately, the first bar or two of a wide range of baroque and classical melodies. If you can get hold of a copy of Barlow and Morgenstern's *A Dictionary of Musical Themes* you will have thousands of fragments to choose from. Begin by finding recordings of works by famous baroque and classical composers (compilation discs such as those that come with magazines such as *The Gramophone* or excerpts downloaded from the Internet are fine). Now look-up these works in Barlow and Morgenstern and try to sing the printed themes. Immediately check how close you are by playing the first few seconds of the corresponding track of the CD. This is not a sight singing exercise, so an approximate rendition will do. If you can't get hold of Barlow and Morgenstern you could use the thematic indexes printed at the start of many albums (such as ABRSM editions of Mozart's and Beethoven's Sonatas and Chopin's Mazurkas). These exercises will not only help you prepare for this test, they will also build an awareness of the musical styles of a number of composers thus helping you give right answers in question (e).

Questions (b) and (c)

These rhythm and pitch tests involve the same sort of skills as test (a) so, even if you decide not to answer (a), you could benefit from practising in the way we have suggested above. It is much easier initially to notate your answers into the skeleton score itself, but remember that you **must** copy them into the staves provided in the answer booklet.

Question (d)

In this question you may be asked to identify modulation to any of the following keys:

From a major key to its:
  tonic minor or relative minor
  dominant or relative minor of its dominant
  subdominant or relative minor of its subdominant

From a minor key to its:
  tonic major or relative major
  dominant or the relative major of its dominant
  subdominant or relative major of its dominant

Most of these types of modulation are included in the six tests in this chapter. You can hear a modulation from a minor key to the relative major on **CD1 track 26** of the accompanying CDs – the music begins in D minor and then modulates to F major, confirmed by a perfect cadence 19 seconds from the start. Other types of modulation can be heard in *Sound Matters* (Schott Educational Publications) as follows:

● from a major key to its subdominant: page 138 (bars 1–8 are in F major, bars 9–11 are in Bb major).
● from a minor key to its subdominant: page 84 (bars 53–56 are in A minor, bars 57–60 are in D minor).
● from a minor key to the relative major of its dominant (i.e. the key on the flat seventh degree of the scale): page 97 (bars 1–6 are in F♯ minor, then there is a perfect cadence in E major in bar 7).

Note that when asked to identify a key in this question you should always give its specific name (e.g. G major) rather than its relationship to the previous key (e.g. dominant).

Questions on chords may involve identifying any of the following:

    I (in root position, first inversion or second inversion)
    II, IV and V (in root position or first inversion)
    III and VI (in root position only)
    VII (in first inversion only)
    V^7 (in root position or any inversion) and II^7b
    the diminished 7th, the Neapolitan 6th and the augmented 6th

augmented 6th   V

You may also have to recognise the standard types of cadence and the circle of 5ths. The Neapolitan 6th is a first-inversion triad on the flat supertonic, and most commonly occurs in minor keys (e.g. a first inversion chord of Db major in the key of C minor). The distinguishing feature of the augmented 6th (shown right) is its interval of an augmented 6th which typically moves outwards to resolve onto the dominant. The other notes of this chord can vary. For more on keys, chords and cadences, see pages 18–32 of *Aural Matters*.

Question (e)

Your commentary can be written in note form or in continuous prose. You are likely to get one mark for each accurate point you make, so if eight marks are available you should aim to make *at least eight* separate points about the extract. There are several other important matters to keep in mind:

● you should concentrate on *significant* features of the music – vague observations that could be true of almost any piece (such as 'it has a steady beat and varied dynamics') are unlikely to gain marks,

● you will not receive credit for repeating the same point in different words (e.g. if you have identified a texture as polyphonic you will not get a further mark for stating that the music is contrapuntal),

● you will not receive credit for mentioning anything that is obvious from the score alone (e.g. stating that the music is 'in triple metre and loud' will not get a mark if the score is marked ¾ and *f*).

● if you refer to a specific event in the music you should give its location (e.g. 'there is syncopation just before the end' or 'there is imitation in bar 12').

Remember that the examiners will be looking for perceptive observations that reveal how much you have heard and understood. General impressions, such as saying the music is exciting, it has a rich texture or that you like the piece, are not required. Our answers at the end of this book are meant to suggest the sort of things that might attract marks *but they are not meant to be exhaustive* (you will learn much by challenging your teacher to suggest other creditable observations).

You are likely to be asked to identify the style, genre and possible date of the music – we have covered some of the important points in this area on pages 47–53.

Remember that this test will need up to 30 minutes to complete – if you decide to tackle it last, make sure that you leave sufficient time. In the actual exam, the score will be printed in a separate insert and the recording will be divided into separate 'tracks', making it easier to locate specific sections for re-play. In this book we have added track times in the first three tests in order to help you locate sections.

Follow the skeleton score printed opposite as you listen to the whole of this track and then answer ANY TWO from questions (a), (b) and (c). You must also answer both (d) and (e). Question (e) is printed after the score. We suggest that you spend no more than 30 minutes on this test.

(a) In which bar does each of the following musical fragments begin?
In each case, write your answers in the spaces provided.

The fragments are not necessarily shown in the order in which they are heard.

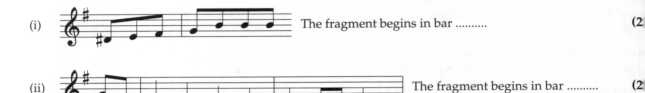

(i) The fragment begins in bar .... (2

(ii) The fragment begins in bar .... (2

(iii) The fragment is heard in bar .... (2

(b) Complete the **rhythm only** of the solo violin part from bar 2, beat 4 to bar 4, beat 3, ignoring the trill in bar 3.

You may work in rough on the skeleton score, but you must copy your answer onto the stave below.

(6

(c) Add **pitches** to the rhythm of the solo violin part from bar 10, beat 4 to bar 12, beat 2.

You may work in rough on the skeleton score, but you must copy your answer onto the stave below.

(6

(d) (i) Identify the **four** different chords marked with arrows in bars 6–7.
Note that the second chord is played twice. The key here is E minor.

1. ....   2. ....   3. ....   4. .... (4

(ii) Identify the key in bars 13–14. .... (1

(iii) Identify the key in bars 20–21. .... (1

(iv) Complete the following sentence:

A harmonic sequence begins at beat .... of bar .... and ends at beat .... of bar .... (2

Turn over

(e) Write a short commentary on this music as directed below.
   You may write in note form, bullet points, or in continuous prose.

   (i)   Comment on any significant features of this music.
         For example: rhythm, melody, harmony, and instrumentation.

   ....

   ....

   ....

   ....

   ....

   ....

   ....

   ....

   ....   **(8)**

   (ii) The music your have heard is the central movement of a work in three movements.
         What sort of composition do you think it comes from?

   ....   **(1)**

   (iii) Place the music in its social and historical context by indicating a possible year of composition,
         a possible composer and the circumstances in which it might have been performed.

   ....

   ....

   ....

   ....

   ....   **(3)**

Total: 32 marks

Follow the skeleton score printed on page 71 as you listen to the first 80 seconds of this track and then answer ANY TWO from questions (a), (b) and (c). You must also answer both (d) and (e).

Question (e) is printed below to save you having to turn the page while answering the other questions, but you should attempt the other questions first.

We suggest that you spend no more than 30 minutes on this test.

(e) Write a short commentary on this music as directed below.
     You may write in note form, bullet points, or in continuous prose.

   (i)   Comment on any significant features of this music.
         For example: rhythm, melody, harmony, tonality, texture and instrumentation.

   ....

   ....

   ....

   ....

   ....

   ....

   ....

   ....

   ....

   .... **(8)**

   (ii) From what sort of work is this extract most likely to have been taken?
         Answer the question by underlining **one** of the following:

   tone poem   **symphony**   **concerto**   **octet**   **(1)**

   (iii) Place the music in its social and historical context by indicating a possible year of composition,
         a possible composer and the circumstances in which it might now be performed.

   ....

   ....

   ....

   ....

   .... **(3)**

Turn over

(a) In which bar does each of the following musical fragments begin?
In each case, write your answers in the spaces provided.

The fragments are not necessarily shown in the order in which they are heard.

(i)  The fragment begins in bar .... **(2)**

(ii)  The fragment begins in bar .... **(2)**

(iii)  The fragment begins in bar .... **(2)**

(b) Complete the **rhythm only** of the melody played by flute and clarinet together in bars 33–36.

You may work in rough on the skeleton score, but you must copy your answer onto the stave below.

 **(6)**

(c) Add **pitches** to the rhythm of the first violin part in bars 13–16. You may work in rough on the skeleton score, but you must copy your answer onto the stave below.

 **(6)**

(d) (i) Describe the bass part in the first four bars as precisely as possible.

.... **(2)**

(ii) In which **one** of the first 8 bars do you hear a minor chord? bar .... **(1)**

(iii) Identify the two chords in bars 7–8. The key here is A major.

chord in bar 7 .... chord in bar 8 .... **(2)**

(iv) Identify the key and the two chords in bars 9–10.

key .... **(1)**

chord in bar 9 .... chord in bar 10 .... **(2)**

(e) **Remember to answer question (e) on the previous page.**

Total: 32 marks

[70]

CD2 track 20

Follow the skeleton score printed opposite and on page 74 as you listen to the first 62 seconds of this track and then answer ANY TWO from questions (a), (b) and (c). You must also answer both (d) and (e). Question (e) is printed after the score. We suggest that you spend no more than 30 minutes on this test.

(a) In which bar does each of the following musical fragments begin?
   In each case, write your answers in the spaces provided.

   The fragments are not necessarily shown in the order in which they are heard.

(i)   The fragment begins in bar .... **(2)**

(ii)   The fragment begins in bar .... **(2)**

(iii)   The fragment begins in bar .... **(2)**

(b) Complete the **rhythm only** of the clarinet part in bars 13–16. You may work in rough on the skeleton score, but you must copy your answer onto the stave below.

(6)

(c) Add **pitches** to the rhythm of the clarinet part from bar 28, beat 2 to the first note of bar 31. You may work in rough on the skeleton score, but you must copy your answer onto the stave below.

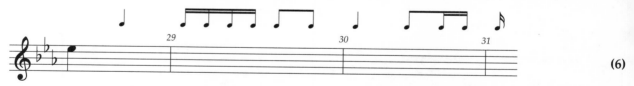

(6)

(d) (i) Identify the **four** chords marked *w*, *x*, *y* and *z* in bars 1–4. The key here is E♭ major.

   1. ....   2. ....   3. ....   4. ....   **(4)**

   (ii) Identify the key of the bracketed passage in bars 11–12. .... **(1)**

   (iii) Identify the key in bars 32–33. .... **(1)**

   (iv) Identify the chords in bars 31 and 36–37 by choosing answers from the following list.

   augmented 6th   **diminished 7th**   **Neapolitan 6th**   **dominant 7th**

   Bar 31 ....   Bars 32–33 ....   **(2)**

[72]

(d) (iii) key?

sf sf   (d) (iv) chord?

(e) Write a short commentary on this music as directed below.
You may write in note form, bullet points, or in continuous prose.

    (i)   Comment on any significant features of this music.
        For example: rhythm, harmony, tonality and texture.

....

....

....

....

....

....

....

....

....

.... **(8)**

    (ii) The piece from which this extract was taken is one of four pieces published together. Consider
        the style and performance directions then underline the title the composer might have given
        to these pieces.

                studies   **characteristic pieces**   **sonatas**   **dances**   **(1)**

    (iii) Identify **three** features of the extract that might lead you to the conclusion that this music is
        late romantic in style.

       1. ....

       2. ....

       3. .... **(3)**

Total: 32 marks

[74]

This test is based on the first 2 minutes 58 seconds of *CD2 track 8*. Listen to the music while following the score printed on page 77. Notice that the first 16 bars are repeated.

Answer ANY TWO from questions (a), (b) and (c). You must also answer both (d) and (e).

Question (e) is printed below to save you having to turn the page while answering the other questions, but you should attempt the other questions first.

We suggest that you spend no more than 30 minutes on this test.

(e) Write a short commentary on this music as directed below.
You may write in note form, bullet points, or in continuous prose.

(i) Comment on any significant features of this music.
For example: rhythm, ornamentation, harmony and tonality, and phrase structures.

....

....

....

....

....

....

....

....

....

.... **(8)**

(ii) Now listen to the **entire track** and then underline the term below that most accurately describes the form of the complete movement.

rondo form   **sonata form**   **binary form**   **ternary form**   **(1)**

(iii) Place the music in its social and historical context by indicating a possible year of composition, a possible composer and the likely instrument(s) for which it was originally intended.

....

....

....

....

.... **(3)**

(a) In which bar does each of the following musical fragments begin?
In each case, write your answers in the spaces provided.

The fragments are not necessarily shown in the order in which they are heard.

(i)  The fragment begins in bar .... **(2)**

(ii)  The fragment begins in bar .... **(2)**

(iii)  The fragment begins in bar .... **(2)**

(b) Complete the **rhythm only** of the melody in bars 25–26. You may work in rough on the skeleton score, but you must copy your answer onto the stave below.

 **(6)**

(c) Add the **pitches** of the melody in bars 30–31. You may work in rough on the skeleton score, but you must copy your answer onto the stave below.

 **(6)**

(d) (i) Identify the chord in bar 2. The key here is G major. .... **(1)**

(ii) Identify the **three** chords marked with arrows in bars 6–8. The key here is G major.

bar 6 ....   bar 7 ....   bar 8 .... **(3)**

(iii) Identify the chord at the start of bar 11. The key here is D major. .... **(1)**

(iv) Identify the key in bar 16. .... **(1)**

(v) Identify the key in bars 23–24. .... **(1)**

(vi) What sort of melodic decoration is used in the bass part in the second half of each of bars 27–30? Answer the question by underlining **one** of the following words or phrases.

arpeggios   **passing notes**   **grace notes**   **appoggiaturas** **(1)**

(e) **Remember to answer question (e) on the previous page.**

Total: 32 marks

[76]

This test is based on the first 87 seconds of *CD1 track 9*. Before attempting the following questions you should listen to the music several times while following the score printed on the next two pages. Note that there are two fast dotted-crotchet beats per bar and that each of the first three sections is repeated.

Answer ANY TWO from questions (a), (b) and (c). You must also answer both (d) and (e).
Question (e) is printed after the score. We suggest that you spend no more than 30 minutes on this test.

(a) In which bar does each of the following musical fragments begin?
In each case, write your answers in the spaces provided.

The fragments are not necessarily shown in the order in which they are heard.

(i) The fragment begins in bar .... **(2)**

(ii) The fragment begins in bar .... **(2)**

(iii) The fragment begins in bar .... **(2)**

(b) Complete the **rhythm only** of the first violin part from bar 10, beat 2 to bar 13a, beat 2.

You may work in rough on the skeleton score, but you must copy your answer onto the stave below.

(6)

(c) Complete the melody in bars 38 to 45 by adding **pitches** to the given rhythms.

You may work in rough on the skeleton score, but you must copy your answer onto the staves printed on page 80.

(d) (i) Identify the key of bars 4–6. .... **(1)**

(ii) Identify the key of bars 8–10. .... **(1)**

(iii) Identify the **three** chords marked with arrows in bars 28–29a. The key here is C minor.

   1. .... 　　　　2. .... 　　　　3. .... **(3)**

(iv) Complete the following sentence:

   A passage in the tonic major begins in bar .... and ends in bar .... **(2)**

(v) What sort of chord can you hear on the second beat of bar 44?
   Answer the question by underlining **one** of the following:

   dominant 7th　　　**diminished 7th**　　　**augmented 6th**　　　**Neapolitan 6th** **(1)**

Allegro molto e vivace

(d) (i) key?

(b) add violin rhythm

(d) (ii) key?

(d) (iii) chords?

Turn over

(c) add pitches to these violin rhythms

(c) add pitches to these violin rhythms

(c) add pitches to these violin rhythms

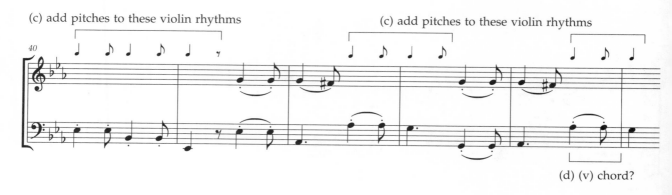

(d) (v) chord?

Write your answer to question (c) on the staves below.

(6)

(e) Write a short commentary on this music as directed below.
You may write in note form, bullet points, or in continuous prose.

(i) Comment on any significant features of this music.
For example: rhythm, melody, harmony, tonality, texture and instrumentation.

....

....

....

....

....

....

....

....

....

.... **(8)**

(ii) The music you have heard is from the third movement of a string trio in four movements.
What title might the composer have given to a movement in this position within a longer
work and with this musical style?

.... **(1)**

(iii) Place the music in its social and historical context by indicating a possible year of composition,
a possible composer and the circumstances in which it might have been performed.

....

....

....

....

.... **(3)**

Total: 32 marks

CD2 track 4

This test is based on the first 1 minute and 46 seconds of *CD2 track 4*.

Answer ANY TWO from questions (a), (b) and (c). You must also answer both (d) and (e).
Question (e) is printed after the score. We suggest that you spend no more than 30 minutes on this test.

(a) In which bar does each of the following musical fragments begin?
     In each case, write your answers in the spaces provided.

     The fragments are not necessarily shown in the order in which they are heard.

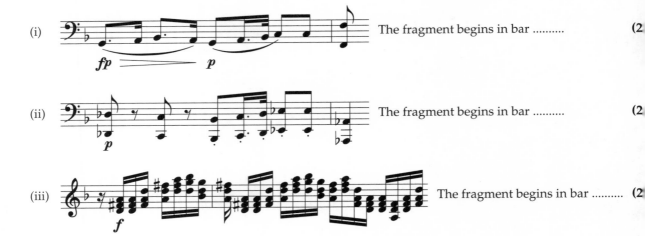

(i)   The fragment begins in bar .... (2)

(ii) The fragment begins in bar .... (2)

(iii) The fragment begins in bar .... (2)

(b) Complete the **rhythm only** of the solo vocal melody in bars 11–13. You may work in rough
     on the skeleton score, but you must copy your answer onto the staves below.

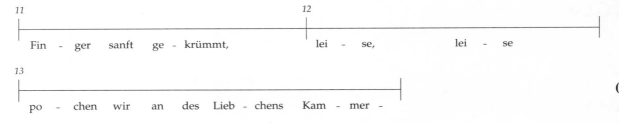

(6)

(c) Add pitches to the rhythm of the vocal melody in bars 20–22. You may work in rough on the
     skeleton score, but you must copy your answer onto the staves printed on page 80.

(d) (i)   With which **one** of the following types of melodic ornament are all the chords in
          bar 3 decorated? Underline your answer.

          passing notes   accented passing notes   acciaccaturas   appoggiaturas (1)

    (ii) Describe the harmonic progression in bars 4–7. .... (2)

    (iii) Identify the key of bar 10. .... (1)

    (iv) Identify the key of bar 11. .... (1)

    (v)   Choosing from the following list, identify chords *x*, *y* and *z* in bars 24–25:

          Neapolitan 6th   augmented 6th   diminished 7th   dominant 7th

          x ....   *y* ....   *z* .... (3)

(d) (i) type of melodic ornament?

semiquavers continue throughout the song

(d) (ii) harmonic progression?

(b) add rhythm of contralto solo

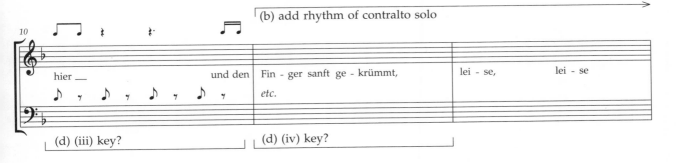

(d) (iii) key?   (d) (iv) key?

Turn over

(c) add pitches to the rhythm of the contralto solo

(d) (v) chord?

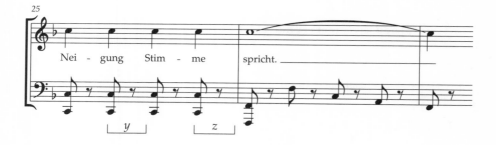

Write your answer to question (c) on the stave below.

(6)

(e) Write a short commentary on this music as directed below.
You may write in note form, bullet points, or in continuous prose.

(i) Comment on any significant features of this music.
For example: melody and text, harmony and tonality, texture and resources.

....

....

....

....

....

....

....

....

.... **(6)**

(ii) Here is a translation of the text of this extract:

Hesitatingly, quietly, in the cover of evening's darkness, we are here;
And with finger gently bent, quietly, quietly
We tap lightly at the loved one's door.
But now rising, swelling, uplifting,
With united voices loudly we call out to her we love:
"Sleep ye not, when the Voice of Love is heard".

Referring to any **four** specific words or phrases in the text, show how the composer has illustrated the poet's ideas in his music. Do **not** refer to the changes in dynamics.

....

....

....

....

....

.... **(4)**

(iii) Place the music in its social and historical context by indicating a possible year of composition and a possible composer.

.... **(2)**

Total: 32 marks

Use the charts below to record your marks as you work through this book.

AS Question 1	AS Question 2	AS Question 3	AS Question 4	AS Totals
Test 1 /9				
Test 2 /9				
Test 3 /9				
Test 4 /9		Test 15 /12	Test 21 /12	
Test 5 /9	Test 10 /12	Test 16 /12	Test 22 /12	/45
Test 6 /9	Test 11 /12	Test 17 /12	Test 23 /12	/45
Test 7 /9	Test 12 /12	Test 18 /12	Test 24 /12	/45
Test 8 /9	Test 13 /12	Test 19 /12	Test 25 /12	/45
Test 9 /9	Test 14 /12	Test 20 /12	Test 26 /12	/45

A2 Question 1	A2 Question 2	A2 Question 3	A2 Totals
	Test 31 /16	Test 37 /32	
	Test 32 /16	Test 38 /32	
Test 27 /12	Test 33 /16	Test 39 /32	/60
Test 28 /12	Test 34 /16	Test 40 /32	/60
Test 29 /12	Test 35 /16	Test 41 /32	/60
Test 30 /12	Test 36 /16	Test 42 /32	/60

Answers

The suggestions below do not represent the only answers that would be acceptable in a public examination. Responses that are accurate and unambiguous, or which refer to different (but valid) points, will receive credit in exams. In the text below an oblique (/) separates alternative answers. Words in brackets are primarily for explanation and are not essential parts of the answer. The marks are for guidance only and do not necessarily indicate the weightings that would be applied in operational papers.

If you get any answers wrong, listen to the music again to ensure that any musical techniques you missed during the test can be recognized *in the recording* once they have been pointed out. In most cases, any unfamiliar terms or concepts can be looked up in the index of our earlier book, *Aural Matters*, which will indicate further examples to be found in the text of that book and illustrated among its associated recordings. Study these, and never be afraid to ask your teacher if you need further help.

Test 1

		Marks
(a)	four	1
(b)	trombone / sackbut	1
(c)	homophonic / chordal	1
(d)	contrapuntal / polyphonic	1
(e)	imitation	1

Source A Biagio Marini (c.1587–1663):
Sonata a quattro tromboni.

(f)	harpsichord (1) any type of lute (1)	
	cello / violone (1)	*max.* 2
(g)	syllabic (1) recitative (1)	2

Source B Vivaldi: 'Tu Judex es' from the oratorio *Juditha Triumphans* RV645 (Venice, 1716). Written to celebrate a Venetian victory over the Turks, the work is sub-titled 'a sacred military oratorio' and is based on the biblical story of Judith's triumph over the forces of King Nebuchadnezzar.

Total **9**

Test 2

(a)	harp	1
(b)	treble / boy soprano (*not* just 'soprano')	1
(c)	melody and accompaniment	1
(d)	three	1
(e)	unison (1) harmony / chords / parts (1)	2

Source A Britten: 'Balulalow' from *A Ceremony of Carols* (1942). Notice the very clear alternation of tonic major and tonic minor chords in the accompaniment, particularly at the start and end of the carol.

(f)	brass / trumpets	1
(g)	quartet	1
(h)	homophonic / chordal	1

Source B Purcell: 'The Queen's Funeral March' from *Music for the Funeral of Queen Mary*. Purcell's score indicates that this march was 'sounded before her chariot' (i.e. horse-drawn hearse) as the great funeral procession made its way to Westminster Abbey on 5th March 1695. It was played again at Purcell's own funeral in Westminster Abbey, where he had been organist, later that same year. The instruments on this recording are 'flat trumpets' – slide trumpets that acquired this name because they could be used in 'flat' (i.e. minor) keys.

Total **9**

Test 3

(a)	octaves	1
(b)	tenor	1
(c)	melody and accompaniment (1)	
	doubles (1) unison (1)	3

Source A Amy Woodforde-Finden (1860–1919): 'Kashmiri Song' from *Four Indian Love Lyrics* (1902). The words are ascribed to 'Laurence Hope' – actually the pen-name of Adela Cory. Originally printed privately because no publisher was interested, the 'Kashmiri Song' quickly became one of the most famous of all Edwardian parlour ballads.

(d)	monophonic	1
(e)	(i) horn	1
	(ii) clarinet / bassoon	1
	(iii) double bass	1

Source B Beethoven: Scherzo from Septet in E♭, Op.20 (1799). The first movement of this work can be found in the *New Anthology of Music* (*NAM 17*).

Total **9**

Test 4

(a)	alternately (allow 'in antiphony')	1
	cello	1
	pizzicato	1
	octave	1
	arco / double- or triple-stopping	1
	piano trio	1

Source A Debussy: Scherzo-Intermezzo from *Piano Trio in G* (c.1879). Written when Debussy was 17, this early work is closer to 19th-century salon music than the impressionist style of his later works, such as *NAM 5*.

(b)	church / cathedral / all-male	1
(c)	imitative	1
(d)	sung unaccompanied	1

Source B Tallis: *Salvator Mundi* I (published 1575). The Latin text suggests that this may have been a pre-reformation (pre-1549) motet. Tallis later turned it into an Anglican anthem by supplying English words. The work demonstrates some of the most characteristic sounds of renaissance church music – modal, imitative and sung by an *a capella* choir of male voices (trebles, male altos, tenors and basses).

Total **9**

Test 5   Marks

(a) oboe (**1**), imitated (**1**), continuo (**1**)   **3**
(b) counter-tenor / male alto   **1**
(c) canonic (**2**) / same melody an octave
    lower (**1**) / imitative throughout (**1**)   *max.* **2**

Source A Handel: 'Be ye sure that the Lord he is
God' from the *'Utrecht' Jubilate* (1713). The *Te Deum*
and *Jubilate* are part of the Anglican morning service
of Mattins, and Handel's settings of both texts were
first sung at St Paul's Cathedral London to celebrate
the 'Peace of Utrecht' – a treaty which concluded a
war with France.

(d) soprano   **1**
(e) they sing in (compound) 3rds / 10ths   **1**
(f) The tenor echoes the higher voice a 10th lower. **1**

Source B Mendelssohn: 'Ich wollt' meine Lieb'
('I want to declare my love to you') from *Six Duets*,
Op.63 No.1 (text by Heine). Composed in 1836.

                                                     Total **9**

Test 6

(a)
(at 0:01) 4-part (SSAT) / all-male / church choir (**1**)
           with organ (**1**) homophonic / chordal
           texture (**1**) and syllabic word-setting (**1**)
(at 0:18) 6-part / extra or bass voices join in (**1**)
           organ more prominent (**1**)
(at 0:54) 3-part (**1**) pairs of voices in thirds (**1**)
           over descending scale in lowest part (**1**)
           antiphonal exchanges (**1**) melismatic
           word-setting (on *cantate* and *exultate*) (**1**)
(at 1:27) imitative entries (**1**)
(at 1:57) contrapuntal texture (**1**)   *Max.* **5**

Source A Monteverdi: *Cantate Domino a 6 voci.*
Published in 1620 the emerging new style of the
baroque is evident in the inclusion of a continuo part
(realised very discreetly on the organ in this recording), dancing triple-time rhythms with syncopation
(hemiolas) at some cadences, mainly homophonic
texture, syllabic word-setting and clear sections
separated by cadences. Compare this with the
flowing renaissance style of Tallis on **CD1 track 6**.

(b) tenor   **1**
(c) melismatic (**1**)
    it is sung to a single vowel sound / ah (**1**)
    broken chords / arpeggios (**1**)   **3**

Source B Reynaldo Hahn (1875–1947) 'La Barcheta'
from *Venezia* (six songs in the Venetian dialect, 1901).
Hahn was born in Venezuela but lived in France,
where he produced a number of works for the stage.
An accomplished singer, he would accompany himself on the piano in songs like this in the fashionable
salons of Paris. *La barcheta* ('the small boat') is cast in
the style of a traditional Italian love-song and tells
the story of a couple being rowed on the Venetian
lagoon by the light of the moon.

                                                     Total **9**

Test 7

(a) string   **1**
(b) (i) chords   **1**
    (ii) arpeggios   **1**
(c) the melody is played by the pianist (**1**)
    the arpeggios are also played by the pianist (**1**)
    the strings now play the chords (**1**)   *max.* **2**
(d) cello   **1**

Source A Ernest Chausson (1855–1899): Sicilienne
from *Concert in D major*, Op.21 (1892). Chausson, like
Hahn (see previous question) had been a pupil of
Massenet at the Paris Conservatoire and later became
a friend and supporter of Debussy. The title 'concert'
reflects the key role given to the solo violin, making
the work more like a small-scale concerto than a sextet.

(b) three   **1**
(c) they have the same rhythm / sing together (**1**)
    they are in parallel 4ths throughout (**2**)   *max.* **2**

Source B Guillaume Dufay (c.1400–1474): Communio
from *Missa Sancti Jacobi*. Dufay was born in Northern
France and became the leading composer of his day,
bridging the transition from medieval music to the
new style of the renaissance. This excerpt illustrates
a common technique of 15th-century church music –
the top part is based on plainsong and the middle
part duplicates this part a 4th lower (such shadow-
ing of parts being known as fauxbourdon).

Test 8

(a) three-part   **1**
(b) viola   **1**
(c) by adding (two) violins /
    by using double- (and/or triple-) stopping   **1**
(d) pizzicato (**1**) dominant pedal (**1**)   **2**
(e) string quintet   **1**

Source A Brahms: Finale of String Quintet No.2 in
G major, Op.111. Composed in 1890.

(f) vibrato (**1**), ostinato (**1**), glissando (**1**)   **3**

Source B Malcolm Arnold (born 1921): *Allegretto
languido* from Flute Sonatina (1948). Arnold played
first trumpet in the London Philharmonic Orchestra
until 1948, thereafter becoming turning his attention
entirely to composing. His many works, often quite
light in character, include more than 80 film scores.

                                                     Total **9**

Test 9

(a) (they sing in) 3rds / parallel motion   **1**
(b) (they double) in octaves   **1**
(c) vocalisation / melismatic   **1**
(d) it plays a (dominant) pedal / monotone   **1**
(e) tenor   **1**
(f) it adds sustained notes (**1**) and then a
    moving bass part (**1**)   *max.* **1**

Source A Reynaldo Hahn (1875–1947): 'Lydie' from
Études latines (1900). See notes on Test 6B. Hahn
dedicated this song to Massenet, his composition
teacher at the Paris Conservatoire.

(g) (bare) octaves   **1**
(h) rising (**1**) staccato (**1**) scales (**1**) in 3rds (**1**)
    over dominant pedal (**1**)   *max.* **1**
(i) melody is now harmonised (**1**) in 6ths (**1**)
    over a (double) pedal (**1**). In addition, the
    accompaniment pattern from the second part
    of the introduction is incorporated (**1**).   *max.* **1**

Source B Xaver Scharwenka (1850–1924): Intermezzo
from *Piano Concerto No.4 in F minor*, Op.82 (1908).
Even in 1908 this charming work must have seemed
old-fashioned in style – notice how so much of the
excerpt presents simple melodies (in octaves, 3rds or
6ths) based on the primary triads (I, IV and V).

                                                     Total **9**

Test 10   **Marks**

(a) A is played by brass instruments alone.   **1**

     B includes one or more percussion instruments.   **1**

(b) timpani / kettledrums (**2**) or drums (**1**)
     (no mark for 'drum')   *max.* **2**

(c) a semitone (**2**) A is higher than B (**1**)
     A is in C♯ minor (**1**), B is in C minor (**1**)   *max.* **2**

(d) A is (much) faster than B   **1**

(e) there are no rests between the phrases in A (**1**),
     the repeat in B is much louder / uses more
     instruments / has a different timpani part (**1**),
     A is played on period instruments while B is
     played on modern instruments (**1**),
     in B the melody is ornamented (**1**),
     the final chord of the first playing is major
     in A (**1**) but an open/bare 5th in B (**1**), there
     is more dynamic shaping of phrases in A (**1**),
     bass doubled an octave lower in B (**1**).   *max.* **4**

(f) use of timpani / slow pace / deep brass
     makes B more ceremonial and dramatic /
     ornamentation makes B more authentic /
     starkness of A makes it more mournful   **1**

                             Total **12**

Source Purcell: 'The Queen's Funeral March' from
Music for the Funeral of Queen Mary. See notes on
Test 2B. No timpani part by Purcell survives – the one
heard in performance B is a modern reconstruction.

Test 11

(a) (i) tenor   **1**

     (ii) (mezzo) soprano, but allow (contr)alto   **1**

     (iii) B   **1**

(b) it is slower (**1**) and the chorus is repeated (**1**)   **2**

(c) a semitone (**2**) A is higher than B (**1**)
     A is in B major (**1**), B is in B♭ major (**1**)   *max.* **2**

(d) chamber orchestra (**1**) symphony orchestra (**1**)   **2**

(e) (i) harpsichord   **1**

     (ii) cymbals / side drum / glockenspiel or
     celesta / horns / trombones / tuba /
     piccolo / flutes / clarinets   **1**

(f) Performance B has thicker instrumentation /
     uses a larger choir / has different part-
     writing in the refrain / has differences in
     ornamentation   *max.* **1**

                             Total **12**

Source Thomas Arne (1710–1787): 'When Britain
first at heav'n's command' from *Alfred* (1740). Sub-
titled 'A grand ode in honour of Great Britain', Arne
wrote the song as the finale to a stage play by James
Thomson, in which it was sung by King Alfred,
glorious in victory over the Danes. Performance A is
of Arne's original version, performance B is of Sir
Malcolm Sargent's arrangement, made originally for
the inauguration of the Royal Festival Hall in 1951
and subsequently often played (as an alternative to
Henry Wood's version) at the last night of the proms.

Test 12

(a) tenor (**1**) piano (**1**) counter-tenor / male alto (**1**)
     harpsichord (**1**) cello / violone (**1**)   **5**

(b) a major 3rd (allow a minor 6th) (**2**)
     A is higher than B (**1**)
     A is in F major (**1**), B is in D♭ major (**1**)   *max.* **2**

(c) more rhythmic variety (**1**), greater variety of
     articulation (**1**), piano has a more soloistic role /
     distinctive counter-melodies (**1**)   **3**

(d) use of / greater dynamic range of piano (**1**) and
     use of unprepared dissonance (**1**)   **2**

                             Total **12**

Source 'Sound the Trumpet', from *Orpheus Brittanicus:
Six duets by Henry Purcell* realized and edited by
Britten and Pears (1961). The original version
(notated in D major and for two counter-tenors and
continuo) comes from Purcell's Birthday Ode for
Queen Mary, *Come Ye Sons of Art*, 1694.

Test 13

(a) A   **1**

(b) D major   **2**

(c) A: horns (and oboes) (**1**),
        violins (allow strings) (**1**),
     B: trumpets (**1**), oboes / double reeds (**1**)   **4**

(d) (i) side drum (**1**)   (ii) harpsichord (**1**)   **2**

(e) more trills / ornamentation in B   **1**

(f) A has large numbers of wind instruments (**1**)
     and no strings (**1**), making it more suitable
     for outdoor performance. Use of harpsichord
     in B indicates it is a performance more likely
     intended for the concert hall (**1**).   *max.* **2**

                             Total **12**

Source Handel: 'La Réjouissance' from *Musick for the
Royal Fireworks* (1749). **CD1 track 1** re-creates the
scale of the work's first performance, with 24 oboes,
12 bassoons, 9 horns, 9 trumpets, 4 pairs of timpani,
a pair of extra large drums, and four side-drums.
Marriner's recording uses the string parts later added
by Handel, and a much more modest wind section.

Test 14

(a) B   **1**

(b) The two performances are at approximately
     the same pitch   **1**

(c) double bass (**1**) pizzicato (**1**) (allow bass guitar
     for **1** mark), snare drum (**1**) with brushes (**1**),
     cymbals (**1**) with drum stick (**1**)   *max.* **4**

(d) Performance B is a jazz (**1**) interpretation and
     there are many differences in rhythm (**1**) and
     ornamentation (**1**). (+ **1** mark for each specific
     difference – e.g. the arpeggiated minor chord
     in the first section is spread downwards in A
     but upwards in B). Performance B includes
     syncopation (**1**) in the drum and bass parts.
     Differences are greater in the second section (**1**)
     in which the swung rhythms (**1**) are heard and
     in which dissonances are added (**1**) to some of
     the chords. When the second section is repeated
     the only significant contrast in A is a lower
     dynamic level (**1**) whereas in B the repeat of
     both sections is much faster / in double time (**1**)
     with a prominent ritardando (**1**) at the end.
     In addition, the melodic material is subjected
     to considerable elaboration (**1**).   *max.* **6**

                             Total **12**

Source: J. S. Bach (1685–1750): Aria from the *Goldberg
variations*. J. G. Goldberg was a keyboard virtuoso and
one of the most talented of Bach's pupils, but whether
this work was really written for him is uncertain. The
aria heard here first appeared in a notebook of pieces
that Bach began collecting in 1725 for his second wife,
Anna Magdalena Bach. Performance A is the original
version, here played on the piano, while Performance B
is of a jazz arrangement by Jacques Loussier.

Test 15

Option A

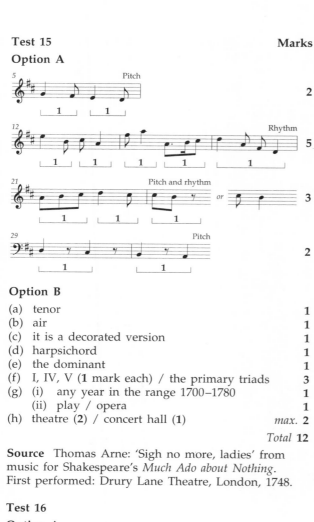

Marks

Pitch — 2

Rhythm — 5

Pitch and rhythm *or* — 3

Pitch — 2

Option B

(a) tenor — 1
(b) air — 1
(c) it is a decorated version — 1
(d) harpsichord — 1
(e) the dominant — 1
(f) I, IV, V (**1** mark each) / the primary triads — 3
(g) (i) any year in the range 1700–1780 — 1
    (ii) play / opera — 1
(h) theatre (**2**) / concert hall (**1**) — *max.* **2**

Total **12**

Source Thomas Arne: 'Sigh no more, ladies' from music for Shakespeare's *Much Ado about Nothing*. First performed: Drury Lane Theatre, London, 1748.

Test 16

Option A

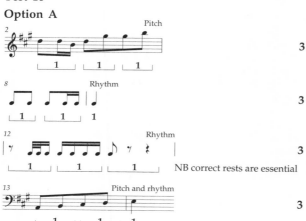

Pitch — 3

Rhythm — 3

Rhythm — 3   NB correct rests are essential

Pitch and rhythm — 3

Option B

(a) (i) (treble) recorders — 1
    (ii) obbligato / solo (**1**) instruments playing ritornelli / similiar music (**1**) at the beginning and end (**1**) and sometimes with the singer (**1**) — *max.* **3**
(b) (i) cello / violone — 1
    (ii) repeated notes (**1**) forming a tonic (**1**) pedal (**1**) — 3
(c) lute (allow any member of the lute family) — 1
(d) cantata — 1
(e) baroque — 1
(f) Bach (allow any German-speaking contemporary, including Handel) — 1

Total **12**

Source J. S. Bach: *Schafe können sicher weiden* ('Sheep may safely graze') from Cantata No.208, *Was mir behagt, ist nur die muntre Jagd!* Known as 'The Hunt Cantata', it was probably written for the birthday of the Duke of Saxe-Weissenfels, 1713. Bach's original is in B♭ major, a semitone higher than the recording.

Test 17

Option A

Pitch — 4   The ♮ sign is essential

Pitch and rhythm — 4

Rhythm — 4

Option B

(a) (i) (chamber) organ — 1
    (ii) any member of the lute family (allow 'guitar') — 1
(b) (i) rhythms are changed — 1
    (ii) ornaments are added — 1
(c) major (**1**) triad (**1**) / tierce de picardie (**2**) — 2
(d) dotted — 1
(e) melodic minor — 1
(f) ground / ostinato — 1
(g) dance (**1**) variations (**1**) — 2
(h) 17th — 1

Total **12**

Source Biagio Marini (*c.*1587–1663): *Romanesca* (published 1620). The *Romanesca* is one of the most famous chord sequences to be used as the basis for variations in the period 1550–1650. It consists of the pattern III–VII–i–V III–VII–(i–)V–i, which Marini has used here in the key of G minor.

Test 18

Option A

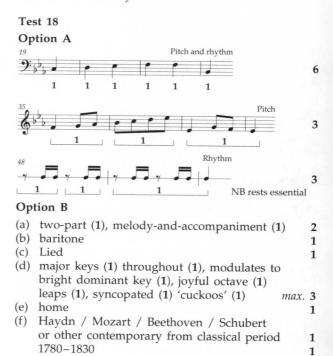

Pitch and rhythm — 6

Pitch — 3

Rhythm — 3   NB rests essential

Option B

(a) two-part (**1**), melody-and-accompaniment (**1**) — 2
(b) baritone — 1
(c) Lied — 1
(d) major keys (**1**) throughout (**1**), modulates to bright dominant key (**1**), joyful octave (**1**) leaps (**1**), syncopated (**1**) 'cuckoos' (**1**) — *max.* **3**
(e) home — 1
(f) Haydn / Mozart / Beethoven / Schubert or other contemporary from classical period — 1
1780–1830 — 1

(g) vocal phrases all four bars long / periodic / balanced (1), (overwhelming) use of primary triads / I, IV, V7 (and their inversions) (1) 2

Total **12**

Source Beethoven: *Maigesang* ('May Song'), Op.52, No.4, believed to date from prior to 1796.

Test 19   Marks

Option A

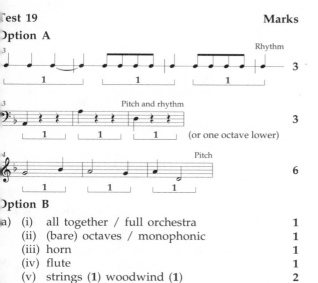

Rhythm 3

Pitch and rhythm 3

(or one octave lower)

Pitch 6

Option B

(a) (i) all together / full orchestra 1
    (ii) (bare) octaves / monophonic 1
    (iii) horn 1
    (iv) flute 1
    (v) strings (1) woodwind (1) 2
(b) unison (1) thirds and sixths (1) 2
(c) call and response (1) strophic (1) 2
(d) 1896 1
(e) operetta 1

Total **12**

Source Sidney Jones (1861–1946): 'Happy Japan', opening chorus from *The Geisha*. First performed in 1896, this operetta achieved even greater success than *The Mikado* (1885). The fashion for all things Japanese was to find its greatest musical expression a few years later in Puccini's opera *Madame Butterfly* (1904).

Test 20

Option A

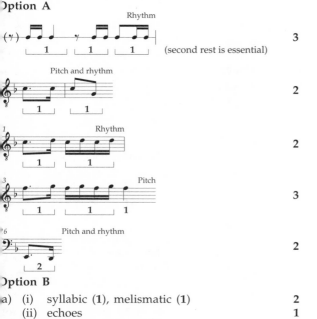

Rhythm 3

(second rest is essential)

Pitch and rhythm 2

Rhythm 2

Pitch 3

Pitch and rhythm 2

Option B

(a) (i) syllabic (1), melismatic (1) 2
    (ii) echoes 1
    (iii) triadic (1), imitates (1) 2
(b) homorhythmic / parts move together (2) / syllabic (1), text repeated (1) *max.* 2

(c) transposes it / modulates to new key / shifts the repetitions by two beats 1
(d) (i) use of ground bass (1), tonal harmony (1) quality of English word-setting (1) *max.* 2
    (ii) use of piano (1), unprepared discords (1) copious performance directions (1) *max.* 2

Total **12**

Source 'Sound the Trumpet', from *Orpheus Brittanicus: Six duets by Henry Purcell* realized and edited by Britten and Pears (1961). For further details see notes on Test 12.

Test 21

(a) major 1
(b) perfect 1
(c) minor 1
(d) different key (1) / minor key (2) *max.* 2
(e) (i) Vb or G/B 1
    (ii) V or G 1
    (iii) Ib or C/E 1
(f) the dominant / G (major) 1
(g) third quaver of bar 17 1
(h) different key (1) / major key (2) *max.* 2

Total **12**

Source Handel: recitative and opening ritornello of the aria 'O, what pleasures' from the oratorio *Alexander Balus* (1747). The two sopranos in the recitative represent Cleopatra and her companion Aspasia.

Test 22

(a) (i) I or F 1
    (ii) Ib or F/A 1
    (iii) IV or B♭ 1
    (iv) II or Gm 1
(b) (i) plagal 1
    (ii) perfect 1
(c) dominant 1
(d) It ends with a perfect cadence in a minor key 1
(e) (i) VI or Dm 1
    (ii) Ic or F/C 1
    (iii) V or C (1) / V^7 or C^7 (2) *max.* 2

Total **12**

Source 'Now thank we all our God' can be found in most traditional hymn books. The melody and words come from the 17th-century German chorale, *Nun danket alle Gott*. The simple harmonisation here is based on the setting that occurs in Mendelssohn's Symphony No.2 ('Hymn of Praise'). It contrasts with Bach's more elaborate settings (*Riemenschneider* 32 and 330) – a point of interest for students offering chorales as a 'techniques' option for A-level music.

Test 23

(a) tonic (1) pedal (1) 2
(b) (i) dominant (1) perfect (1) 2
    (ii) dominant (1) interrupted (1) 2
(c) (i) relative minor 1
    (ii) dominant 1
(d) (i) Ic or B♭/F 1
    (ii) V$^{(7)}$ or F$^{(7)}$ 1
(e) 29 (1), 32 (1) 2

Total **12**

Source Beethoven: Scherzo from Septet in E♭, Op.20 (1799). The first movement of this work can be found in the *New Anthology of Music* (*NAM 17*).

Test 24

		Marks
(a)	(i) major triad (**1**) root position (**1**)	2
	(ii) major triad (**1**) first inversion (**1**)	2
	(iii) minor triad (**1**) first inversion (**1**)	2
(b)	modal (**1**) major (**1**)	2
(c)	dominant	1
(d)	imperfect	1
(e)	It modulates.	2
	Total	**12**

Source C. V. Stanford (1852–1924): 'The Chapel on the Hill', from *A Fire of Turf*, Op.139 (1913).

Test 25

(a)	minor	1
(b)	(i) I / Gm	1
	(ii) V / D	1
(c)	(harmonic) sequence (**1**) circle/cycle of 5ths (**2**)	*max.* 2
(d)	chromatic (**1**) scale (**1**)	2
(e)	(i) Ic or Cm/G	1
	(ii) V$^{(7)}$ or G$^{(7)}$	1
	(iii) I or Cm	1
(f)	diminished 7ths	1
(g)	tonic	1
	Total	**12**

Source Vivaldi: 'Agitata infidu flatu' from *Juditha Triumphans* RV645 (Venice, 1716), the composer's only surviving oratorio. Like so many of his works, it was written for the girls of the Pietà, the Venetian orphanage where Vivaldi was director of music. The score includes a number of unusual instruments, including the *chalumeau*, an early type of clarinet.

Test 26

(a)	(bar 3) minor (**1**), (bar 4) major (**1**)	2
(b)	(first chord) VI or A♭	1
	(second chord) ivb or Fm/A♭	1
(c)	(bar 6) major (allow V or G)	1
	(bar 7) minor (allow v or Gm)	1
(d)	(i) minor	1
	(ii) perfect	1
(e)	(key) relative major (**1**), (cadence) perfect (**1**)	2
(f)	*x* is major / it is a tierce de Picardie (**1**) *y* has no 3rd / it is a bare/open 5th (**1**)	2
	Total	**12**

Source Purcell: 'The Queen's Funeral March' from *Music for the Funeral of Queen Mary*. See Test 2B.

Test 27

(a)	study	1
(b)	it concentrates on one idea/figure (playing rapid 3rds and 6ths) throughout	1
(c)	1899	2

Source A Saint-Saëns: *Six Études*, Op.111 No.1 (1899).

(d)	classical	1
(e)	balanced/periodic/4-bar phrases (**1**), clarity of textures (**1**), functional harmonies (**1**), use of small orchestra with clarinets (**1**)	*max.* 1
(f)	Beethoven (**2**) or other Viennese classical composer (Haydn, Schubert etc.) (**1**)	*max.* 2

Source B Beethoven: 'Da stiegen die Menschen an's Licht' from *Cantata on the Death of Emperor Joseph II* (1790).

(g)	It is from a cantata written for performance in a concert hall by an amateur choir	1
(h)	19th	1
(i)	dissonant / complex harmonies (e.g. V^{13}) (**1**) large orchestra (**1**)	2

Source C Hamish MacCunn (1868–1916): 'O Caledonia! stern and wild' from *The Lay of the Last Minstrel*, Op.7 – a cantata composed for the Glasgow Choral Union in 1888.

Total **12**

Test 28

(a)	lied	
(b)	Schumann (**2**) or Schubert / Brahms / Wolf (**1**)	*max.* 2
(c)	1810–1890	

Source A Schumann: *Sänger's Trost*, Op.127 No.1 (1840).

(d)	church / cathedral / all-male	
(e)	anthem	
(f)	Purcell	

Source B Purcell: Hear My Prayer (*c*.1681).

(g)	American country music / bluegrass / folk fiddle / accept country and western	
(h)	20th-century orchestral work	
(i)	use of syncopation (**1**), jazzy rhythms (**1**), large brass section (**1**), use of xylophone / modern percussion instruments (**1**)	*max.* 2

Source C The Arkansas Traveller: Old Fiddlers' Breakdown (the arrangement is anonymous but the original melody dates back to at least 1854).

Total **12**

Test 29

(a)	concerto	
(b)	romantic	
(c)	it is very fast (**1**), very difficult (**1**), technically brilliant (**1**), showy (**1**)	*max.* 2

Source A Xaver Scharwenka (1850–1924): Intermezzo from *Piano Concerto No.4 in F minor*, Op.82 (1908).

(d)	lied	1
(e)	Schubert (**2**) or Schumann / Brahms / Wolf (**1**)	*max.* 2
(f)	domestic performance in the home	1

Source B Schubert: 'Auf dem Flusse' from the song cycle *Winterreise* (1827).

(g)	waltz	1
(h)	1890–1900	1
(i)	use of chromaticism (**1**) and rubato (**1**)	2

Source C Alexander Glazunov: *Petite Valse*, Op.36 (1892).

Total **12**

Test 30

(a)	post-modernism combination of open 5ths and discords / static rhythm / hummed choral parts / meditative / simple repetitive patterns (sequences) / modal	1
(b)	sacred music	1
(c)	1969	1

Source A Georgy Sviridov (1915–1998): 'Sacred Love'. A pupil of Shostakovich, Sviridov avoided Communist prohibition of religious music such as this by writing it under the guise of 'incidental music' for the theatre.

d) second / slow   1
e) jazz   1
f) any year from 1920 to 1970 inclusive (**2**)
    or any other year in the 20th century (**1**)   *max.* 1

Source B Malcolm Arnold (born 1921): *Allegretto languido* from Flute Sonatina. See notes on Test 8B.

g) character piece   1
h) for performance in the home   1
i) romantic   1
j) emphasis on melody (**1**) with dense (**1**) and arpeggiated (**1**) accompaniment comprised of many 7th chords) / tonal dissonances (**1**). Tendency to modulate towards ii and IV more than V (**1**). Use of much rubato (**1**).   *max.* 1

Source C Georgy Catoire (1861–1926): *Loin du foyer* ('Far from home'), No.2 of *Trois morceaux* Op.2 (*c*.1888). Catoire was a Russian of French descent. His studies with Rimsky-Korsakov resulted in the three short pieces of his Opus 2. He became a noted teacher at the Moscow Conservatoire, numbering Kabalevsky among his pupils.

Total **12**

Test 31   **Marks**

(a) (i) false (**1**)   (ii) false (**1**)   (iii) false (**1**)
   (iv) false (**1**)   (v) true (**1**)   (vi) false (**1**)   6
(b) (i) excerpt B is a variation of excerpt A   1
   (ii) excerpt B uses mostly the same harmonic patterns as excerpt A   1
(c) Byrd   2
(d) it has more decoration / shorter notes (**2**) (divisions = +**1**), it slows down at the end (**1**), it has a scalic, not triadic, opening (**2**) it includes a non-diatonic pitch / flat 7th the harmony different near the end (**2**)   *max.* 6

Source William Byrd (1543–1623): 'Wilson's Wild' (entitled 'Wolseys Wilde' in the *Fitzwilliam Virginal Book*). This short work is in the form of variations on a popular tune of Byrd's time.

Total **16**

Test 32

(a) (i) 1888 (accept any date from 1850 to 1900)   1
   (ii) it was composed at about the same time   1
(b) for soprano voice (**1**) basically strophic (**1**) use of appoggiaturas (*etc*) for expressive effect (**1**) chromatic harmony (**1**) homophonic texture (**1**) repetitive patterns in accompaniment (**1**) syllabic word-setting (**1**) verse 1 doesn't end on tonic (**1**)   *max.* 3
(c) (i) A (**1**)   (ii) A (**1**)   (iii) B (**1**)
   (iv) B (**1**)   (v) B (**1**)   (vi) A (**1**)   6
(d) A is major while B is minor/modal (**2**)
   A has arpeggiated accompaniment while B has repeated chords (**2**)
   A modulates only to the dominant while B modulates to a variety of keys (**2**)   *max.* 4

Source A Reynaldo Hahn (1875–1947): *Si mes vers avaient des ailes!* ('If my verses had wings'). This exquisite miniature was written in 1888, when Hahn was only thirteen years old. See notes on Test 6B.

Source B Gabriel Fauré (1845–1924): *Après un rêve* ('After a Dream'), composed in 1878.

Total **16**

Test 33

(a) 1675–1700   2
(b) Excerpt A is in the same key as Excerpt B   2
(c) A is homophonic (**1**) B is contrapuntal (**1**)
   A is 4-part texture (**1**) B is 8-part texture (**1**)
   ('B is a thicker texture than A' = **1**)   *max.* 4
(d) perfect (**1**) an open / bare 5th (**1**)
   perfect (**1**) an open /bare 5th (**1**)   4
(e) A is for brass but B is for voices (**1**)
   A has phrases separated by cadences / rests (**1**) while B is seamless / overlapping / imitative (**1**)
   B has greater rhythmic variety than A (**1**)
   A contains only one discord (**1**) while B has many dissonant (**1**) and chromatic (**1**) passages.
   A is repeated while B is not (**1**)   *max.* 4

Source A Purcell: 'The Queen's Funeral March' from *Music for the Funeral of Queen Mary* (1695). See notes on Test 2B.

Source B Purcell: Hear My Prayer (*c*.1681).

Total **16**

Test 34

(a) Liszt   1
(b) 1835 (accept any date from 1810 to 1860)   1
(c) A   1
(d) (i) true (**1**)   (ii) true (**1**)   (iii) false (**1**)
   (iv) false (**1**)   (v) false (**1**)   5
(d) (i) played by the pianist's right hand   1
   (ii) played by the pianist's left hand   1
(e) Excerpt B has more octave doublings (**1**) especially of bass notes (**1**), thicker-textured chords (**1**), a different accompaniment rhythm below the main melody (**1**), much additional decoration in the middle section (**1**) and octave transpositions (**1**) towards the end. There is greater use of rubato in Excerpt A (**1**) and A was recorded live before an audience (**1**).   *max.* 6

Source A Rossini: 'La Regata Veneziana' from *Soirées Musicales* (*c*.1835).

Source B Liszt: 'La Regata Veneziana' transcription for piano (1838).

Total **16**

Test 35

(a) tonic (**1**) dominant (**1**)   2
(b) (i) true (**1**)   (ii) false (**1**)   (iii) true (**1**)
   (iv) false (**1**)   (v) false (**1**)   (vi) true (**1**)   6
(c) (i) trills (**1**) dominant pedal (**1**)   2
   (ii) all the note-lengths are the same   1
   (iii) (an octave) lower (**1**) played in 6ths (**1**) now a tonic pedal (**1**)   *max.* 2
(d) Long notes divided into dotted patterns (**1**) of passing notes (**1**), played an octave lower (**1**)   3

Source A J. S. Bach (1685–1750): Aria from the *Goldberg* variations. See notes on Test 14.

Source B J. S. Bach (1685–1750): Variation 28 from the *Goldberg* variations. Transcribed for strings by Dmitry Sitkovetsky.

Total **16**

Test 36   **Marks**

(a) (i) BOTH (**1**)   B (**1**)   A (**1**)
     BOTH (**1**)   A (**1**)   B (**1**)   6
   (ii) transposed up (**1**) by a (major) 3rd (**1**)   2
   (iii) transposed down (**1**) by a tone (**1**)   2

(b) in A the orchestra continues (**1**) but the dynamic is quieter (**1**) while in B the piano enters (**1**) and the orchestra merely plays isolated chords (**1**). A uses chords I and V (**1**) while B is based on V(7) only (**1**).
A is diatonic (**1**) while B is chromatic (**1**).   *max.* **2**

(c) A persistently repeats the motif (**1**) in balanced phrases (**1**) over pedal points (**1**) and simple root-position harmonies (**1**) while B extends/develops the motif (**1**) chromatically (**1**) and with different rhythms (**1**)   *max.* **3**

(d) chromaticism keeps the listener guessing at the key centre (**1**), fanfare-like interruptions from the wind signal an important event (**1**) the early entry of the piano is unexpected (**1**) constantly fluctuating ideas create a sense of unrest and anticipation (**1**)   max. **1**

Source A Xaver Scharwenka (1850–1924): Intermezzo from *Piano Concerto No.4 in P minor*, Op.82 (1908).

Source B Liszt (1811–1886): first movement of *Piano Concerto No.1 in E♭ major* (1855).

Total **16**

Test 37   **Marks**

NB Answer any **two** *from (a), (b) and (c).*

(a) (i)   4   2
    (ii) 18   2
    (iii) 8   2

(b) [music notation] ½ **1 1 1 1 1** ½   6

(c) [music notation] ½ **1 1 1 1 1** ½   6

(d) (i)   Ib or Em/G   1
          IV or Am   1
          Ic or Em/B   1
          V or B   1
    (ii) B minor   1
    (iii) E minor   1
    (iv) beat 1 bar 17 to beat 2 (or 3), bar 18   2

(e) (i)   **Rhythm**: (solo) dotted rhythms (**1**) including Scotch snaps (**1**), on-beat (**1**) detached (**1**) bass notes with off-beat (**1**) upper string parts, soloist treats rhythm very freely (**1**).
          Melody: diatonic (**1**), appoggiaturas (**1**), balanced/periodic/4-bar phrases (**1**), sighing/weeping appoggiatura figures near the end (**1**), prominent use of harmonic minor scale (**1**).
          Harmony: tonal (**1**), diatonic (**1**) apart from chromatic (**1**) discords (**1**) near the end, mainly primary triads (**1**) and dominant 7ths (**1**).
          Instrumentation: string orchestra (**1**) with horns (**1**) and continuo (**1**)   *max.* **8**
    (ii) (violin) concerto   1
    (iii) 1740–1780   1
          Haydn / Mozart / Linley or other early-classical composer such as Arne, Boyce, J. C. Bach, C. P. E. Bach etc.   1
          small concert hall / theatre   1

Total **32**

Source Thomas Linley the Younger (1756–1778): Adagio from *Violin Concerto in F*. Born in Bath in the same year as Mozart, Linley was as prodigious as his more famous contemporary and was playing violin concertos in public by the age of seven.

Thomas Linley met Mozart in 1770 in Italy, where the two boys at once became firm friends. Linley reputedly wrote more than 20 violin concertos before his death in a boating accident at the age of 22 – this is the only one that survives complete. The original score of this movement was written in F minor, and is transposed down a semitone in this recording.

Test 38

NB Answer any **two** *from (a), (b) and (c).*

(a) (i)   13 or 17
    (ii) 27
    (iii) 35

(b)
    1   **1**   **1** **1** **1**   **1**

(c)
    1   **1**   **1** **1**   **1** **1**

(d) (i)   tonic (**1**) pedal (**1**)
    (ii) (bar) 6
    (iii) (bar 7) V⁷ or E⁷ (**1**)
          (bar 8) I or A (**1**)
    (iv) (key) A minor (**1**)
          (bar 9) V⁷b or E⁷/G♯ (**1**)
          (bar 10) I or Am (**1**)

(e) (i)   **Rhythm**: Lilting effect produced by crotchets on second quaver beat (**1**), subtle use of dotted rhythm (**1**), syncopated accompaniment near end (**1**).
          Melody: lyrical (**1**) but with chromatic notes (**1**) and 4-bar/balanced/periodic phrases (**1**). Use of appoggiaturas (**1**) and sequence (**1**) in bars 9–12, counter-melody in bass (**1**) at bar 13, melody shared between bass and treble (**1**) in the second half.
          Harmony: predominantly primary triads (**1**) and dominant 7ths (**1**).
          Tonality: use of tonic minor (**1**) and modulations to both related and unrelated keys (**1**).
          Texture and instrumentation: chamber orchestra (**1**) with woodwind solos (**1**) although 1st violins and cellos have most melodic interest (**1**). 2nd violins accompany with repeated notes (**1**) and the violas with broken chords (**1**). Horns sustain harmony notes (**1**). Soloistic wind textures at end (**1**).   *max.*
    (ii) symphony
    (iii) 1800–1840
          Schubert (**2**) Beethoven / Mendelssohn / Weber or other composer working in 1821 (**1**)   *max.*
          Public concert in a concert hall

Total **3**

Source Schubert: Andante from *Symphony in D*, D708a (1821). This symphony was one of a number of works that Schubert left unfinished when he died at the age of 31. However, Schubert completed 685 bars in outline piano score, which Professor Brian Newbould orchestrated and completed in 1981. It is that reconstruction which was used for the recording from which this excerpt is taken.

Why Schubert did not complete the work is unknown. Perhaps he felt that prospects of a performance were (as always for his orchestral music) too unlikely, but Newbould suggests that Schubert possibly felt the style was developing on rather old-fashioned lines compared with the emerging romanticism of some of his other works of the 1820s.

Test 39   Marks

NB *Answer any* **two** *from (a), (b) and (c).*

(a) (i)   5   2
     (ii) 17   2
     (iii) 20   2

(b) [musical notation]   6

1 1 1 1 1 1
accept any note longer than a quaver for final note

(c) [musical notation]   6

½ mark per note

(d) (i) w: II^{7}b or Fm^7/A♭   1
           x: Ic or E♭/B♭   1
           y: V^7 or B♭^{7} 1
           z: V^{7}b or B♭^{7}/D   1
     (ii) F minor   1
     (iii) G minor   1
     (iv) bar 31: diminished 7th   1
           bars 36–37: dominant 7th   1
(e) (i)   **Rhythm**: steady quaver bass (**1**) supports
           various dotted (**1**) and syncopated (**1**)
           patterns (e.g. bars 15–16). The basic
           pulse is frequently modified by the
           use of rubato (**1**) and pauses (**1**).
           Harmony: functional (**1**) with some
           chromatic (**1**) discords (**1**) and
           frequent use of 7th chords (**1**).
           Tonality: major (**1**) with frequent
           brief modulations (**1**) sometimes
           to distantly related (**1**) keys.
           Texture: melody and accompaniment (**1**)
           with piano providing counter-
           melodies (**1**).   *max.* **8**
     (ii) characteristic pieces   **1**
     (iii) lyrical melody (**1**) but quite complex
           harmony / many seventh chords (**1**), tonal
           but with wide-ranging modulations (**1**),
           use of wide range (**1**) for both instruments
           much rubato (**1**) written in score (**1**) many
           detailed performing directions (**1**)   *max.* **3**
                                               Total **32**

Source: William Hurlstone (1876–1906): Intermezzo from *Four Characteristic Pieces* for clarinet and piano (*c.*1900). Hurlstone, like his contemporaries Holst and Vaughan Williams, studied composition with Charles Villiers Stanford (represented on CD2 track 19).

These four pieces have become favourite teaching works for the clarinet and often appear in graded examinations.

Test 40

NB *Answer any* **two** *from (a), (b) and (c).*

(a) (i)   8   2
     (ii) 21   2
     (iii) 25   2

(b) [musical notation]   6

1 1 ½ 1 1 ½

(c) [musical notation]   6

1½ 1½ 1½ 1½

(d) (i)   Vb or D/F♯   1
     (ii) bar 6: IIb or Am/C   1
           bar 7: V^7 or G^7 1
           bar 8: I or G   1
     (iii) VI or Em   1
     (iv) D (major)   1
     (v)   E minor   1
     (vi) passing notes   1
(e) (i)   **Rhythm**: wide variety of patterns (**1**)
           including dotted (**1**), reverse dotted /
           Scotch snap / Lombardic figures (**1**)
           and equal semiquavers (**1**), plus equal
           quavers / 'walking bass' (**1**) near end.
           Ornamentation: wide variety (**1**) of French-
           style (**1**) ornaments, including upper (**1**)
           and lower / inverted (**1**) mordents (**1**),
           falling (**1**) and rising (**1**) appoggiaturas
           (**1**), turns (**1**), trills (**1**), slides (**1**) and
           arpeggiated chords (**1**). Examiners will
           also accept appropriate foreign terms
           such as *nachschlag* (bar 2) or *style brisé*
           (broken chords in left hand part).
           Harmony and tonality: mainly diatonic
           (**1** + **1** for each specific exception) and
           functional (**1**) with clear cadential
           progressions (**1**) + **1** for each specific
           example). Modulations to related keys
           (**1**) + **1** for each specific example.
           Circle/cycle of 5ths (**1**) firmly re-
           establishes tonic at the end (**1**).
           Phrase structures: 4-bar / balanced /
           periodic (**1**) phrasing throughout (**1**)
           defined by clear cadences (**1**) + **1** for
           each specific example.   *max.* **8**
     (ii) binary form   **1**
     (iii) 1700–1750   **1**
           (J. S.) Bach, Handel, Couperin   **1**
           clavichord / harpsichord   **1**
                                               Total **32**

Source: J. S. Bach (1685–1750): Aria from the *Goldberg variations*. Bach here uses the term aria (song) to mean a texture in which melody predominates. See the notes on Test 14 for further details.

Test 41   Marks

*NB Answer any **two** from (a), (b) and (c).*

(a) (i)   31   2
     (ii) 20   2
     (iii) 18   2

(b) [music notation]   6

(c) [music notation]   6

(d) (i)   Eb (major)   1
     (ii) G minor   1
     (iii) 1. Ic or Cm/G   1
           2. $V^{(7)}$ or $G^{(7)}$ 1
           3. I or Cm   1
     (iv) (bar) 29(b) (1) (to bar) 34 or 35 (1)   2
     (v)   augmented 6th   1

(e) (i)   **Rhythm**: pervasive use of a short
           rhythmic motifs (1) such as the
           crotchet–quaver figure (1) and the
           quaver–2 semiquaver–quaver figure (1)
           in the opening sections. Prominant
           syncopations (1).
           Melody: triadic (1), largely diatonic (1)
           with some chromatic notes (1).
           Harmony: functional (1) with prominent
           chromatic (1) discords (1).
           Tonality: minor (1) with modulations to
           related keys (1), tonic major (1) and
           relative major (1) near the end.
           Texture and instrumentation: solo violin,
           viola and cello/string trio (1),
           multi-voice chords (1) achieved by
           double/triple stopping (1),
           unaccompanied violin solos (1),
           homophony (1) and dialogue (1),
           with a passage in octaves (1) for all
           three instruments.   *max.* **8**
     (ii) Scherzo (and trio)   1
     (iii) 1780–1830   1
           Haydn/Beethoven/Schubert   1
           Chamber music played in the home   1
                                          Total **32**

Source: Beethoven: Scherzo (and trio) from the
String Trio in C minor, Op.9 No.3. Beethoven's three
Opus 9 string trios were composed in Vienna in
1797–8. The intense, gruff mood, created through the
pervasive use of short rhythmic motifs in a minor
key, is one of the composer's most characteristic
fingerprints.

Test 42

*NB Answer any **two** from (a), (b) and (c).*

(a) (i)   20   2
     (ii) 13   2
     (iii) 18 (allow 19)   2

(b)    6

(c) [music notation]   6

(d) (i)   appoggiaturas   1
     (ii) circle/cycle of 5ths (2)
           harmonic sequence (1)   *max.* 2
     (iii) C (major)   1
     (iv) D minor   1
     (v)   x augmented 6th   1
           y diminished 7th   1
           z dominant 7th   1

(e) (i)   **Melody and text**: the text is divided into
           short phrases (1) in which the solo
           voice is echoed by a chorus (1). Word-
           setting is almost entirely syllabic (1).
           Harmony and tonality: chromatic (1),
           alternations of major and minor forms
           of the same triad (1) with frequent
           appoggiaturas (1) and modulations to
           both related (1) and unrelated (1) keys.
           Texture and resources: solo (contr)alto (1),
           and four-part (1) male-voice chorus (1)
           (TTBB = 2) often heard in dialogue (1)
           with the soloist. Homophonic (1) piano
           accompaniment (1) includes a few
           melodic fragments in the bass (1).   *max.* **6**
     (ii) Detached/staccato articulation of the piano
           part (1) and short vocal phrases (1) suggest
           hesitating movement. The repetitive motif
           in the accompaniment creates a mood of
           stillness (1) while its constant semiquaver
           rhythm suggests the light tapping (1) on the
           door. The words 'rising' and 'uplifiting' are
           illustrated by rising (1) intervals and the
           word 'loud' (*laut*) is strengthened by the use
           of syncopation (1). The idea of united voices
           is conveyed by the soloist and choir singing
           together in the same rhythm (1) for the first
           time. The cry of 'Sleep ye not' is under-
           pinned by an interrupted cadence (1) which
           uses the surprising progression of V^7–bIII (1).
           The 'voice of love' is illustrated by warm,
           chromatic harmony (1).   *max.* **4**
     (iii) 1810–1897   1
           Schubert/Schumann/Brahms or other
           contemporary composer of lieder   1
                                          Total **32**

Source: Schubert: *Ständchen* (Serenade) D.920 (1827).
Anna Fröhlich, a teacher at the Vienna Conservatoire
of Music asked the poet Franz Grillparzer to write
the words, and his friend Schubert to compose the
music, for this song. It was intended to be performed
by her pupils as a birthday surprise for one of their
number. When Schubert presented the male-voice
choir version performed here it was pointed that all
the pupils concerned were girls. The genial Schubert
immediately obliged by not merely transposing the
work, but totally re-writing it for female voices.